GOD'S GRACE IN MARRIAGE

by
Josephine
Kyambadde

MINISTRY IN ART PUBLISHING
The Seal of Excellence

Ministry In Art Publishing Ltd
Email: publishing@ministryinart.com
www.miapublishing.com

This publication is designed to provide accurate and authoritative information in regard to the subject matter covered. It is sold with the understanding that the publisher is not engaged in rendering legal, accounting, or other professional service. If legal advice or other expert assistance is required, the services of a competent professional should be sought.

All scripture quotations taken from KJV, NKJV, TMB, NIV and NLT

ISBN: 978-0-9560996-2-4

Cover design by Allan Sealy
www.miadesign.com

DEDICATION

I dedicate this book to Pastor Funke Adejumo, Pastor Yemi Adeleke, Pastor Yemisi Ashimolowo, Bishop Peter and Pastor Sarah Morgan, Pastor Benedicta Olagunju, Pastors Clem and Marjorie Esomowei, Evangelist Norah Mayanja and to many other pastors not mentioned here. I have sat under your teachings, you have indeed impacted on my life through your words of wisdom. You are living epistles.

My marriage is blossoming because you availed yourself to be used by God. Eternity will celebrate you because of the many lives and marriages you have ministered to.

You will fight a good fight and finish the race. You will be crowned on that day by our Lord Jesus Christ. Well done.

To those who feel like throwing in the towel, stand still, you will see the deliverance of the Lord. The 'Egyptians' you see today, you will never see them again. Hold your peace, carry your cross, you will win the race and receive your crown on that day.

And to those who are divorced, you are not failures. God has forgiven you. He loves you with an everlasting love. His grace is sufficient for you. Learn from your mistakes and keep focused on your call. Fulfill your destiny and the purpose of your living.

Shalom!

With lots of love,

Josephine.

ACKNOWLEDGEMENTS

My wonderful husband Peter Kyambadde,
we have come a long way; indeed, we have witnessed
the gracious hand of God in our marriage.

You are a man of wisdom, love and forgiveness. You're
one in a million! I cherish you and admire you for
being so humble; you are always willing to say these
five letters "SORRY", and that is humility. Your words
are said with grace and sincerity of heart; you touch
my heart and challenge me.

Thank you for loving me and allowing me the freedom
to fulfil my destiny in life. I appreciate that you have
never been a stumbling block in my life. You have
always supported and encouraged me to serve the
Master Jesus Christ. You are my confidant and best
friend. When I am ministering, you cheer me and
make me feel special. I salute you great man of valour.

Our relationship reminds me of the cartoon "Tom and
Jerry"; one minute they fall out another minute they're
great friends. Thank you for allowing me to be me.

Wow! What can I say to our anointed daughter and
sons. Lilly, you have stood with me through thick and

thin - thank you. This book was made possible because of you. You spent sleepless nights to make sure this book becomes a blessing to millions through your gift of writing, typing and editing. Well done!

Davis, your typing skills are beyond words. Surely your fingers are anointed and thanks for the prayers and prophecies that you gave me regarding this book; you will impact on your generation my dear. I declare that your head will never lack any oil (and by this I mean the anointing).

Derrick, my son, I love you. Thanks for the many cuddles you gave me while I wrote this book. Your warmth took away the stress which helped me to finish it. You're a gem.

My nephew Danny, do you know that your smiles kept me going as I typed? God bless you.

Little nephew Azariah, thank you for making your baby noises and seeking attention. Whenever I lift you up and we both smile, I feel happy inside. You have helped me to realise that I needed a break, and when I did get back to writing this book I felt fresh and revived.

My dear sisters and brothers: Grace, Robina, Christine, Ronald, Charles, Joseph, Charles Kijambu and Dorothy; you have made life easy for me by standing with me in all ways. God will help you to fulfil your own dreams also. You have all helped and contributed to destiny.

My brother in-law Paul, you're like your namesake Apostle Paul. Great man of God, my intercessor and friend; may the Almighty God meet your heart's desire, and may you live to leave a positive mark on this earth.

I extend my sincere thanks to my adopted and spiritual daughter Joy and Sister Dora. Your continuous prayers and fasting have pushed me this far.

Thank you to all my treasured co-workers in Christ, Pastor Benedicta Olagunju, Pastor Annena Maria Goreti, Pastor Janet Ribeiro-Addy, Pastor Grace Shola and Pastor Bim Folayan; you went the extra mile to make sure this vision is birthed. I cannot forget the many calls you continually made to encourage me. To your prayers and financial support, I give tribute.

Last but not least, I want to say thank you to all my partners and members of Latter Rain Ministries. You know how much I love you but I want to say it again,

"I LOVE YOU." You guys are so unique, you're quality people, you make work easy for me. You're God's battle axe, and I believe that God will use you to shake nations.

FOREWARD

Josephine and I met in January 1986 at a place nicknamed "Half-London" in Kampala, Uganda. We were both in our early 20s so you can imagine the intensity involved in our love for each other. I was by then an army officer. Two things stood out uniquely about her; her beauty and they way she spoke. Those two among many were irresistible.

All went on well in the early days for needless to say, both of us were at our best behaviour. On the 31st October 1987 we tied the knot.

Our relationship has gone through a lot experience, intense fellowship – just to express it humbly, war of words and the like. As she states in the book, forgiveness and being able to seat and talk over the differences in opinion has kept the marriage going.

We gave our lives to God in 1991 with Josephine leading the way and I following suit. The author is a determined lady with a heart for marriages, women and those hurting. Because of what our marriage has gone through, quarrels, shouting, and separation to mention but a few, it enhances the title of the book and I can surely affirm that indeed it is the grace of God that the marriage is still on. Remember like many other marriages we did not have what you would call proper Christian counselling.   There is also the rift that nearly put us apart because when she got saved she fledged almost immediately as she got committed 100% as for me I was a little bit cautious!

Josephine has applied herself selfishly to the body of Christ and reaching all in conferences, seminars, workshops, radio and TV programmes and offering both marital and premarital counselling to many in the United Kingdom, USA, Uganda, Tanzania, Kenya, Rwanda, Nigeria, Ghana, Gabon and she continues tirelessly to be of service to many no matter the denomination or background.

I continually admire her zeal to reach and help people. It is not unusual to find Josephine in the living room watching news (she's a woman who wants to be informed all the time), the laptop is on – typing either an article for a magazine, a message or working on her new release, the blackberry is on she is replying to someone's e-mail and the landline or mobile phone goes and she still attends to the caller!!! Wow thanks God for the grace of technology as well. Having said all that, she knows how to strike a balance. She properly plans her day, creates time for Prayer, runs around for shopping, prepares hot meals for the family, and finds time for our teenagers and not forgetting the big boy "ME". I find this quite challenging.

I can assure you "God's Grace for Marriages" is packed with useful information based God's word, experience and inspiration from the Holly Spirit. Without a doubt there are many books out there on marriages but I can assure you this one is special and my prayer is that it will change and the way some people think about marriages, salvage many and inspire many to march down the isle and say "I do" confidently knowing that God's Grace In Marriages is real and readily available to all. Please read the book from the beginning to the end and recommend it to someone.

Peter K
(Husband, Pastor - LRMI)

CONTENTS

CONTENTS

INTRODUCTION

Even the best things in life have room for improvement. You may feel you have a fairly strong relationship with your spouse and that your marriage is in fact a good one; even if that is the case, you can still improve on it. Anthony J. D'Angelo said, "Never stop learning; knowledge doubles every fourteen months. Learning stops when you are dead."
Research shows that 78% of the marriages breaking up are Christian marriages. The divorce rate of Christian marriages is alarming! Our marriages are meant to be testimonies before the world. God initiated marriage right from the beginning of time. It was the first institution He established. We may achieve some success in building our homes, but whatever we build will not last, as long as God is not involved in it. Like the Psalmist says, "Unless the Lord builds the house, they labour in vain who build it; unless the Lord guards the city, the watchman stays awake in vain." Psalms 127:1 NKJV

Marriage is hard work. It's not for lazy people. Divorce is not the answer to a troubled relationship - full-stop. The only exception is in cases of extreme mental or physical abuse. Everyone, whether man or woman, has a weakness; there is no couple out there with a perfect, stress-free relationship 100% of the time. Throughout the years of my marriage, I have learnt that it takes the Grace of God for a man and woman to live together. I have seen the grace of God see me through thick and thin. Joyce Meyer said, "Salvation, the infilling of the Holy Spirit, fellowship with God and all victory in our daily lives is based upon Grace." If you wish to enjoy your marriage, ask God for more grace everyday. Without God's grace in my life I would be miserable and hopeless. Let us not forget that it took Grace for you and I to be saved (Ephesians 2:8-9). And yes, it will also take increasing measures of grace for us to stay happily in our marriages.

The reason I am writing this book is because God led me to write something that would touch all those whose marriages are falling apart, and to educate those who are considering the prospect of entering a marriage. Secondly, after ministering at workshops and conferences, men and women have approached me enquiring whether I have a book that covers what I have just preached about marriage.

Sadly, many churches are still not dealing with real issues in marriage, even with christian divorce being such huge problem. As a result, many marriages are suffering, when they could be helped. Many Christians pursue get in marriage before seeking premarital counseling; and some do not all sufficient time, and consequently, many of these marriages have ended up in destruction. I strongly believe that you are reading this book for a reason, and the chances are He wants to deal with you personally, so that your marriage can grow and blossom as it should. God has a timely message for you; He is well equipped to bring perfect order out of the chaos, and can create beauty out of ashes.

In this book you will learn that intimacy does not develop overnight. Being committed and spending quality time together will lead to you eventually build a good marriage. It takes a strong committment to continue in your marriage, even when your partner fails you in some way. The devil will tempt you with suggestions like 'Give up, this marriage will not work', if and when that challenge confronts you need to stand firm on your covenant vows and be determined to endure. Endurance should be your anchor when the tornado of life's storms comes knocking at your door. When Peter and I first fell in love, we grew closer and closer, and then made a solid commitment to each other. As the years have passed we have matured in our understanding of each other to an extent that in most cases we know what one another is thinking and feeling without a word ever having to be spoken. But this didn't develop overnight. Like Anthony J. D'Angelo said, "Treasure your relationships, not your possessions."

It is clear that Christian marriages are under attack. The first love is gone; there's no longer true love. The aim of writing this book is to give you hope that it is not too late to work on your marriage. If you want your marriage to survive, you will need to be willing to work hard on it. Be reassured that the grace of God is upon your marriage. Even the most damaged marriages can turn around for the better, and become healthy. Satan the enemy will use every trick in the book to sabotage your marriage; but God's unfailing grace will see you through every trial, and support you to a successful end. Even though the enemy wants to sabotage your marriage, the grace is there to support you.

According to The Daily Mirror "the law allowing same-sex couples to enter civil partnerships came into action in December 2005 and it is estimated that by 2010 nearly 22,000 homosexual 'marriages' will have taken place." The enemy is attemtping to destroy Godly marriages by encouraging people to embrace homosexuality as a normal union; thus undermining the plan and purpose of God for holy matrimony.

Whether you find yourself dating, married, or engaged you will need the grace of God, the wisdom of the Holy Spirit, and the counsel of mature Christian couples to support you. God has a plan and purpose for your marriage, which is why He has led you to read this book.

The burning question is, why do marriages experience so many problemse? There are obviously some things we don't know yet, some things we have yet to understand; for we know in part, and we prophesy in part (1 Corinthian 13:9). I believe it is not by accident that you are reading this book today. I believe God wants to open your eyes so that you too may avoid failure in marriage, and so that you may experience a breakthrough, and a glorious marriage that God intended. I thank you for allowing me the privilege of being a part of your marriage as I impart words of wisdom that I hope will enrich your marriages, greatly.

If you read the following pages with a willing heart and practice the things you learn in the chapters that follow, you will experience God's power that will make a new marriage blossom into a strong union, resurrect a troubled marriage, and that will see you all the way to your golden anniversaries where you will discover that God has saved the best for the last. And surely He does save the best for last! My husband, Peter, for many years has been encouraging me to write this book because marriages have always been an important part of our ministry. I have counselled couples and individuals, studied dozens of marriage books and attended seminars. But my greatest encouragement to write about marriage is God Himself. By His grace I have been married to Peter for 20 years. He makes me believe I can accomplish anything. He is my confidant, and my best friend. I want to appreciate him, for encouraging me in every thing I do.

My prayer for you is that by the time you finish this book, you will understand God's perfect will for your marriage, and you will be encouraged and be able to stand against the attacks of the enemy that will come against you and your spouse. In Jesus' name.

Shalom!

Chapter 1

MARRIAGE: GOD'S IDEA

"And the LORD God said, it is not good that the man should be alone; I will make him an help meet for him. And out of the ground the LORD God formed every beast of the field and every fowl of the air; and brought them unto Adam to see what he would call them: and whatsoever Adam called every living creature, that was the name thereof. And Adam gave names to all cattle, and to the fowl of the air, and to every beast of the field; but for Adam there was not found an help meet for him." Genesis 2:18-20

Marriage was God's idea from the very beginning. "I will make him a help meet (suitable, adapted, and complementary) or qualified for him." Genesis 2:18. Since man was made a social creature, it was not ideal that he should be alone; for to be alone, without a companion, was not good. Therefore God came up with a good idea that would solve this problem. Marriage is the oldest institution known to man; it dates back to our creation and the Garden of Eden.

God himself preformed the first marriage ceremony, and it was He who gave away the first bride. Scripture reveals that one of God's basic purposes for marriage is companionship. Therefore, it is your duty to be the primary companion of your spouse.

The uniqueness of God's intended companionship in marriage is demonstrated by Adam's difficulty finding a 'suitable' creature to complement him, amongst the many animals he was commissioned to name. To be a good companion you must be suitable for, and compatible to your spouse. In the midst of all the abundance and amusement, that surrounded Adam, he was conscious of feelings he could not gratify. for this reason, God caused a deep sleep to fall on Adam, then presented him with a Eve; a companion and help meet for him. We can see that one of God's purposes for marriage was to make two people happy. He knew that by sharing life together they could taste its richest joys. True companions stand alongside one another, and share their personal and intimate lives together.

It is clear that marriage was God's idea and not man's. That is why we are to acknowledge Him and invite Jesus in our marriage and invite Him to be apart of it. Since He instituted it, He knows how best to make it work. Look at the wedding at Cana:

"And the third day there was a marriage in Cana of Galilee; and the mother of Jesus was there: and both Jesus was called, and his disciples, to the marriage.

༄༅

"THEY TRAVEL LIGHTLY WHOM GOD'S GRACE CARRIES."

-THOMAS KEMPIS-

And when they wanted wine, the mother of Jesus saith unto him, they have no wine. Jesus saith unto her, woman, what have I to do with thee? mine hour is not yet come. His mother saith unto the servants, whatsoever he saith unto you, do it. And there were set there six waterpots of stone, after the manner of the purifying of the Jews, containing two or three firkins apiece. Jesus saith unto them, fill the water pots with water. And they filled them up to the brim. And he saith unto them, draw out now, and bear unto the governor of the feast. And they bare it. When the ruler of the feast had tasted the water that was made wine, and knew not whence it was: (but the servants which drew the water knew;) the governor of the feast called the bridegroom, and saith unto him, every man at the beginning doth set forth good wine; and when men have well drunk, then that which is worse: but thou hast kept the good wine until now. This beginning of miracles did Jesus in Cana of Galilee, and manifested forth his glory; and his disciples believed on him. John 2: 1-10

What was the problem? Who solved the problem? Where did the people take the problem? There was no wine. The wine ran out. Wine is a symbol of the anointing of the Holy Spirit. Some marriages have run out of the anointing. And the only way to get back the anointing of the first love is to come to Jesus and let him minister to you. He knows where you went wrong and He is able to fix your marriage wherever it is broken. Jesus solved the problem. He's the author and finisher of our faith. He is the beginning and the end. When He starts something He will accomplish it. He is the Alpha of your marriage and He is the Omega of your marriage. As long as your marriage was started on the solid Rock of Jesus, He will sustain it. As long as you have known the truth and have decided to commit your marriage to him, He will sustain, bless, and revive it. The first miracle Jesus performed underlines the importance of marriage to God. If you invite Jesus in your marriage, He will solve every problem that is bothering you; and will cause your marriage to blossom.

Mary was present, but could not solve the problem at hand. Jesus is the answer to every problem. No one else can help you. Religion can not help you; or your friendly and family. They may try - and sincerely so -

but they are all limited. Jesus however, is unlimited.

We thank God for Mary. She carried Jesus in her womb for nine months, but she can not solve our problems. Neither can witch doctors, nor palm

> ❧
> "A STATE OF MIND THAT SEES GOD IN EVERYTHING IS EVIDENCE OF GROWTH IN GRACE AND A THANKFUL HEART."
> -CHARLES G. FINNEY-

readers offer us the help we need. Mary's response to the servant was say to the servant? "What ever he says to you, do it."

Because God initiated marriage He made available to us the grace to be able to live successfully with each other. It is important to understanding that you will need grace to enter into marriage; without it will not be able to mangage. God is a God of grace Grace. And He will give you the grace to make your manage a success. He is faithful, don't give up. No marriage is without its problems. Couples that longevity of relationship together have simpy learned how to solve their issues; and how to live with their individual difference.

"But the God of all grace, who hath called us unto his eternal glory by Christ Jesus, after that ye have suffered a while, make you perfect, establish,

strengthen, settle you" 1 Peter 5:10

God is the God of grace, but what you have to know is that He has put that grace there to prepare you for the battles you will go through in your marriage. That's why He says after you have suffered a while; He will make you perfect, establish, strengthen, and settle you. There will be suffering in our marriages but God assures us that He will give us the grace to endure, and after that He will make sure He establishes us, and settles us in our marriages. I pray that you will settle in Jesus' name. Don't give up, and do not grow weary in doing good (2 Thessalonians 3:13).

WHAT IS GRACE?

Grace is God's unmerited favor. Both 'grace' and 'favor' in the New Testament (King James Version) are always a translation of the same Greek word, charis (khar'ece), which translates to, God's unmerited favor. Its first definition in Strong's Greek Lexicon is "graciousness...of manner or act." And it is of interest to note that Webster's Ninth Collegiate Dictionary puts as its first definition of grace, "unmerited divine assistance given man for his regeneration or sanctification." So grace is favour; unmerited favor.

Because you received Christ as your personal savior,

God's grace is available for you if you receive it by faith. If you received Christ by grace through faith, then you can also receive His grace; it is a gift. "...*by grace are ye saved through faith; and that not of yourselves: it is the gift of God.*" *Ephesians 2:8*

We grow in grace as we live together; encourage each other along our life journey. As you allow God's grace to work in both you and your partner, you will finish the race of your marriage, victoriously together. "They travel lightly whom God's grace carries." Thomas Kempis.

By the grace of God you can stay in a difficult marriage, raise a difficult child or even stay at a trying job. Have you been trying to solve your problems on your own? If so, make a change today. Start asking God for His grace. Before you know it your inner man will be strengthened. Paul realised the power of asking when he prayed for the Ephesians to be strengthened in the inner man by the power of the Holy Spirit.

The Spirit of grace will help us in our marriages. That's why we need Him; everyday and for every situation that we encounter. When in trouble He is ever present, so welcome Him into your life. One of the symbols of the Holy Spirit is the anointing oil.

You need the oil of the Holy Spirit in your marriage to bring happiness, peace, and a fresh love. Oil lubricates, and we need the anointing oil to lubricate our marriages and relationships. During difficult times, gives the Holy Spirit opportunity to lead you, by seeking His counsel, before you do or say anything to your spouse. This is the dispensation of the Holy Spirit, so ask God for more grace; remember it is His pleasure to give it to you. He ordained marriage. God is the one who designed marriage.

God He is the mastermind behind the marriage idea; He designed it and He ordained it. Therefore he has a plan for how marriage works best; like the manufacturer of a Toyota car has the best idea how to fix it, God also knows how to repair your marriage if it breaks down.

"A state of mind that sees God in everything is evidence of growth in grace and a thankful heart."
Charles G. Finney

Chapter 2

CHRISTIAN COURTSHIP

Our loving heavenly Father, wants the very best for us in every area of our lives. And our love relationships are no exception. Courtship creates the opportunity for two individual of the oppoiste sex to learn how best to relate. God cares about how two people in a relationship relate to one another. It is the perfect time for you to build a relationship bond with someone, and helps you to understand a persons personality and assess their character. The point is to have fellowship together. In this stage of your relationship, work on nurturing the growth of your love, and eventually this will lead you into a promising start to your marriage. Remember to have fun when you are fellowshipping together. The grace of God is there for you, and as you pray with one another you will become comfortable and happy in each others presence.

While you are still single, be careful not to allow peer pressure to force you into dating situations that are inappropriate. It is common for non-Christians in the world who do not have Christ in their lives to have a distorted view of what dating is about. The most popular worldly ideas about dating is contrary to God's original plan and what He intended for us to experience in courtship. During courtship, some people hide certain unfavourable things about themselves; others even lie just to win someone over. This kind of recreational dating is mostly about self-gratification, dating to satisfy your own needs; without placing enough importance on godly principles of honesty, integrity and truth.

In recent years the word dating has been losing it's meaning; which is why I prefer using the word courtship. Many have been wounded emotionally through worldly dating. Often, dating couples open themselves up, unadvisedly, and sadly get hurt as a result. They give their hearts away believing that they will get something real and worthwhile only to find somewhere down the road the relationship was not what they had hoped for. In some cases, people have been used, which can be devastating for anyone.

Sadly some people date to pass the time, whilst others are in it for the long haul. This is why it is very important to pray that God reveals to you the intentions of the person you are dating. Problems can and do surface in courtship.

Whether in courtship or dating there shouldn't be romantic interaction until after the commitment of marriage, which should always follow a wedding ceremony - never before! This is a rule from God; and His rules birth success

The Bible gives us some very clear principles to guide us in making decisions about courtship. True courting should only happen once and should end in a life-long covenant. It has been said that, "Courtship is about open and honest exploration of each other's lives and families leading to engagement and marriage." In relation to Christian courtship, it has been said that, "Christian courtship examines biblical principles, examples and precedents and applies them to the process of finding a spouse and getting married. The result involves some of the principles of "traditional" courtship, along with some deletions and modifications."

I have seen people dating and have even witnessed some people dating more than one person. This always ends in tears and emotional scaring for the un-knowing person. Very rarely can someone with such habits have an exclusive relationship. The worldly term for this is "player"- someone who effectively plays with people's emotions and lies to them whilst seeing other people. Though some "players" are successful in fooling their partners, this does not last and eventually people get the strength to leave them and move on. It's very hard for someone who is a "player" to have a marriage that actually lasts. From my point of view dating can make you vulnerable. Dating is like marriage, but without the protection. You go out together, spend time together, and give your hearts to each other with no life-long commitment, and with no covenant. And then when it goes wrong you wonder why you get hurt. We must learn to relate according to the marriage covenant. This is the boundary that protects our 'sphere of vulnerability'.

Courtship seeks to emulate the godly models described in the Bible. Dating is different, and is worldly in nature. My belief is that we should follow God's model, because it is the most effective and fulfilling way to have a successful marriage. Nevertheless, do not be discouraged. God's grace will see you through any temptations and crossroads you may experience. Courtship is biblical. It is a model for the relationship leading up to marriage. In the Bible, parents were always involved in the marriage process. However, they did not arrange the marriage without their children's consent. See Genesis 24:57-58. "We will call the young woman and ask her personally." Then they called

Rebekah and said to her, "Will you go with this man?" This is a clear example that shows Rebekah had a choice and her parents also had involvement in her choice. This is what God wants us to do. And she said, "I will go." Although they were certainly involved in the arrangements, sometimes the parents went out and found partners for their children; and then the children were consulted for their opinion, thoughts and feelings. Other times a young man would approach the father of his beloved and make his intentions known. We will see this issue in more details later on.

You cannot choose a romantic mate without knowing fairly and intimately the person who your heart is fond of. That is why courtship is good and necessary. When you are courting, invite one another to your homes, worship together, go to conferences together; and in everything you do pay attention to one another. By this I mean discover each other's likes and dislikes, take note of one another's reactions in different situations. It is good and even recommended not to rush courtship, the more you discover about one another the better. It has been said "rushing the ingredients of a recipe makes a bad cuisine." So take your time and make sure you make the right decision, because it will affect you for the rest of your life.

Court someone who brings out the best in you. I have noticed when a person is courting in the will of God, better qualities come out. There is contentment, a smile, a willingness to help people, not hurt people. No wonder the Bible says, "House and riches are the inheritance of fathers: and a prudent wife is from the LORD" (Proverbs 19:14). *"Whoso findeth a wife findeth a good thing, and obtaineth favour of the LORD" (Proverbs 18:22).*

Brothers, I start by addressing you. Do not commit yourselves to a marriage partner until you're emotionally, spiritually and materially prepared for marriage. Be prepared financially for marriage; have a steady job and save for your future wife, so that your family can enjoy a nice lifestyle. It is fundamentally important to also have an honest and intimate relationship with God. This helps you make the right decisions when picking a wife.

For my dear sisters, a similar set of criteria should first be achieved before you consider yourselves ready for courtship and marriage. Emotionally and spiritually you should also strive for maturity, waiting with patience and faith in God for the right brother that will bring out the best in you, whilst you as a wife fulfil all your duties to him (Ephesians 5:22-24, 30-33).

The reason why marriages are breaking down is because people enter into marriage without really knowing each other. Remember, you are different; you are from different backgrounds, you have different minds (opinions) and most likely different education. This is why you need to get to know each other's characteristics. You need to prepare adequately. Preparing is a process that everybody should go through before marriage.

"Call unto me, and I will answer you, and show you great and mighty things, which you know not."
Jeremiah 33:3

In this scripture, God promised to reveal things. He will reveal to you the right time to get married, reveal things about your fiancé, life, job, and even give you direction and insight.

Dating and letting young ladies down is evil. This has been done, time and time again, and the results have been indescribably painful. Terrible emotional wounds have been inflicted on countless lives; no wonder many girls don't want to get married, and they live in insecurity. I organised a conference and a crusade in Uganda, where a young lady pastor came to me at the end and said, "I have been delivered today. I was in a relationship, we were dating but I was sexually abused. So I decided I will never get married. I had hatred towards all men. But when I heard your message, why God ordained marriage, my eyes were opened. I received a clear revelation of marriage, I am free today. I am now ready to get into marriage, I have received forgiveness, and I have forgiven." She was so happy, praise the Lord. She was completely delivered by hearing God's word.

THINGS TO CONSIDER FOR COURTSHIP

There are four things I recommend that you give consideration to:
- Look
- Book
- Hook

and

- Take

Let us delve a little deeper to explore what these words represent.

LOOK

It is okay to look around and see what you want. Don't rush into dating the first person that you see and like. Rather, look around and pray for God's guidance, like you would go out for shopping. You first go around and see what you want, after deciding what you want you put a deposit, or book it. Pray, but keep your eyes wide open to see who you want; be specific and articulate your desires to God. I once heard Pastor Adeboye from Redeemed Christian Church tell a story of a sister who wanted a husband and she told God to give her anybody, and she would take him as a husband. One day a brother came up to her and said, "Thus saith the Lord, I am your husband," the sister went back to God and told Him, "God I didn't tell you to give me anything but anybody." What a joke!

As you look around, guard your heart. The Bible tells us to be very careful about giving our affections, because your heart influences everything else in our life. "Above all else, guard your heart, for it is the wellspring of life" (Proverbs 4:23).

I believe it is not easy to find a mate; it takes the grace of God. Some people go hunting in churches. By doing this they become spiritual tourists and this is not right, because they are not pastored by anyone specifically. So they are indeed more likely to make the wrong decision. Others use the internet (Christian dating sites). God works in mysterious ways. I cannot deny the fact that you can get a godly fiancé on the internet. It can happen. I have heard of many couples who are happily married through this. However, I would recommend that you pray about it, and also plan to visit each other. But all in all, look up to God; and stay in your church. God is able to bring your partner to you. Do not panic!

Friendship

Let your relationship start from a friendship and grow into a committed engagement, then onto marriage. Use the courtship to become friends. Identify common denominators (i.e. same interests and objectives, etc). Honor, value and respect each other. You will come to know each other fairly well and you will become good friends, and in the end you will begin to grow fond of one another. You will discover whether your partner is grounded in the word; for example, if you have an argument how do they react? Are they always furious, filled with anger? If so, pray seriously about moving forward. If there is no change, then you will need to change your plans because we are told in God's word,

"Do not make friends with a hot-tempered man, do not associate with one easily angered, or you may learn his ways and get yourself ensnared" Proverbs 22:24-25.

Be careful! You don't want a partner who will strip you of your identity and drain you spiritually.

"Two are better than one, Because they have a good reward for their labor. For if they fall, one will lift up his companion." Ecclesiastes 4:9-10

When you are in courtship, do not seclude yourself or the relationship. This creates unnecessary and avoidable temptations. Stay in public places and even involve friends in some of your meetings.

Another thing to look out for is if your friends celebrate your achievements, if not, then something is wrong. For example, if you're a man and your lady has a better job and therefore a higher income, rejoice with her. If you are too insecure to do so, and think that her achievements will cause you to lose control; remember that it is not God's will that a man control a woman - and vice versa. Ultimately, whatever He does to bless your spouse, He can also do for you.

"Then Jethro rejoiced for all the good which the Lord had done for Israel, whom He had delivered out of the hand of the Egyptians." Exodus 18:9

A true friend will celebrate with you.

LOVE

As you pray and look around for Mr or Miss Wonderful, the Lord will lead you to someone. But how do you know when you've found the right mate? Agape love should be your driving force. The Bible says about love in 1 Corinthians 13:4-7. We ought to love someone for who they are; love their strength and pray for their weakness. Be patient with each other. Let the unconditional love of God be in both of you. When the true love of God is in you, you will be kind to each other and will not keep a record of wrongs. That is an indication of real love. Be honest with your partner because honesty is an expresion love. You should have your partners' best interests in mind. This means keeping yourself pure, and preparing resources for a stable marriage, etc. This brings us to our next point.

BOOK

Once you have made up your mind about what you want to buy, you now book it by placing a deposit on it. It is a similiar principle at work when you have identified who you want to court. If you're a man, now is the time to mention it to your prospective partner, and ask her to many you. Look for a special place to share your feelings. If she accepts then you progress into an engagement.

Ladies, when a brother tries to propose to you and you feel led to commit yourself to him, don't quickly get excited and say yes, or else it will look as if you have been desperately waiting for someone. Instead, your response should be to ask him to wait while you consult God and get back to him to confirm. If a brother asks you to go out, when are making arrangement to meet, instead of responding with a keen "yes, I'm available," try saying "I need to first check my daily to see if am free that day." Even if you know for sure that you're free, do not mention it to him. Then when he calls you back to confirm, that is when you agree to go with him, but when you do go out, stick to public restaurant or any other public place. You don't want to go to his house where you could fall into temptation. You need to go away and spend some time to get to know each other. You may not feel love straight away, you may not feel anything about him in the early stages, but don't let this put you off, go and meet him anyway. If God has revealed that this is the right person, do not give up too easily. Abraham Lincoln reportedly said, *"I don't like that man. I must get to know him better."* As you pray and you continue to go out with each other, you will get to know each other better, and grow in an understanding of the qualities that are not immediately as you hoped they would be.

If you dine while courting, when you get in the restaurant be careful the way you eat, and what you say, it will speak volumes to your prospective partner. And even when you finally have become so close to each other and he decides to meet his parents, be careful the way you walk, talk and eat. His parents are studying you; they are watching to see what type of sister you are and if they feel comfortable with you marrying their son.

These days people bump into each other, immediately they feel a spark of chemistry, they fall in love and after a few weeks they tie the knot with a spectacular wedding event. Down the road they encounter problems and true colors come out, as they inevitably do. When such couples begin experiencing mental issues with each other, because they failed to build a foundation; what was a rushed wedding, ends in divorce. It is so important that you take time to know someone. You don't want to end up so frustrated in your relationship that you abuse your spouse. Some men have been known to treat their wives as slaves; and some wives can be so controlling and disrespectful that they hurt their husbands and destroy his self esteem and confidence. My sister and brothers, if you fall into any of those categories, as you read this book you need to repent and change your ungodly ways and cruel character. Such abusive behaviour, if dealt with in court could result in you losing your right to see your children, let alone the loss of the marriage itself.

SPIRITUAL MATURITY

As a Christian it is important that you court someone who brings you closer to God. Exodus 20:3 says, *"Thou shalt have no other gods before me."* God intends all binding relationships to draw us closer to Him, never to become an idol that takes us away from Him. This has to be one of the great tests of a genuine, God sent, made-in-Heaven courtship, which leads to marriage. Ask yourself "Does the person I'm courting bring me closer to God?" If they are taking you out of service from God and taking your heart from God, then something needs to be re-evaluated quickly.

It is imperative to marry someone who is growing in maturity, and by that I mean someone who loves God and has a relationship with Him. Do they respect their pastor? Are they submissive? It would be good for you to visit their church if you do not attend the same church; and whilst there, make arrangements to meet the pastor, if possible, or an elder. Does the person that you're considering for marriage attend church regularly? Do they contribute to the church ministry? Do they tithe often? You will find out the truth about their spiritual maturity as you talk more and learn about each other. Ask God to reveal to you everything you need to know about your prospective spouse. Before you get married make a mutual commitment to growing in the spirit. Pray, read your bible, and exercise the fruit of the Holy Spirit together. support each other in your Christian duties.

PURITY

Court in purity. Paul said to Timothy, "...keep thyself pure" (I Timothy 5:22). He also said to the Thessalonians, *"For this is the will of God, even your sanctification, that ye should abstain from fornication: That every one of you should know how to possess his vessel in sanctification and honour." 1 Thessalonians 4:3-4*

PARENTS

After you have been with someone for a fair period of time you need to come to a decision. Make up your mind, either end the courtship, or progress to the next stage. Otherwise if you fail to make a definite decision you will be in danger of falling into sin by prolonging the opportunity for you to be tempted. If you decide to advance from a courtship to an engagement, it is a great honour to receive the blessings of all the parents concerned. One of the great blessings in life is the gift of parents. As a rule, you cannot be right with God and wrong with your Mom and Dad. The Scriptures show us that the blessing is two-fold in honoring our parents. First, your life is prolonged and secondly, it goes well with us. Your life will not be blessed if it runs contrary to the biblical pattern of blessing. You should seek to get the green light from your parents before you go ahead. **You need parental authority and blessing.**

Ladies, let me draw your attention to what the bible says concerning you. *"So then he that giveth her in marriage doeth well; but he that giveth her not in marriage doeth better."* 1 Corinthians 7:38

We see that God intends for a father to give his daughter away. This is more than symbolic. This is an appointment made by God, not man. The Lord Jesus said, *"For this cause shall a man leave his father and mother, and cleave to his wife; And they twain shall be one flesh: so then they are no more twain, but one flesh. What therefore God hath joined together, let not man put asunder"* Mark 10:7-9.

By biblical principle a young man is under the same obligation as a young lady to secure the blessing of the parents. *"And Abraham said unto his eldest servant of his house, that ruled over all that he had, Put, I pray thee, thy hand under my thigh: And I will make thee swear by the LORD, the God of heaven, and the God of the earth, that thou shalt not take a wife unto my son of the daughters of the Canaanites, among whom I dwell: But thou shalt go unto my country, and to my kindred, and take a wife unto my son Isaac"* Genesis 24:2-4.

There are repercussions that can come from courting and marrying outside the blessings of the parents. You can become like the prodigal's son.

When a child goes away from the upbringing of his godly youth and willfully chooses to stay in the "far country," he will encounter inevitable eventualities that will make him run into trouble, thereby making him return home.

"And not many days after the younger son gathered all together, and took his journey into a far country, and there wasted his substance with riotous living. And when he had spent all, there arose a mighty famine in that land; and he began to be in want" Luke 15:13, 14.

If you don't repent, you may find yourself living in a prolonged state of "want." The word want comes to us from a Greek word, *hustero,* which means inferior in power, influence or rank or to lack excellence.

If you have already gone ahead of your parents and got married, find comfort in Christ. When we confess any past wrong-doing, *"He is faithful and just to forgive us our sins and cleanse us from all unrighteousness"* 1 John 1:9.

HOOK

After you have known each other six months or more, you may now plan to get engaged. This is the stage of the courtship I call the Hook. At this point you need to be transparent with each other, on a much deeper level than before. Be honest, if you have a child your partner needs to know; pray about it, ask God to lead you in finding the best time to mention it to the one you seek to marry. Normally this is not an easy thing to do, but if you are willing to go ahead with an engagement, pray about the issues and then leave them to God. Remember to love your partner the way they are because love conquers all things.

I have seen many couples who entered in marriage and failed to be honest to their spouses and when the truth came out which it always does, the marriage ends in seperation. Withholding truth will seriously damage the trust that your partner had for you. It is so important to be open; if you have debts, let your partner know.

In some parts of Africa, the man pays the dowry to the lady's family. Paying a dowry before marriage shows that you are serious and you respect the parents of your wife to be. The whole process is overseen in a protective and guiding manner by the parents involved; this also reduces both emotional and physical threats from the dating process, and actually prove to enrich the engagement.

"Honor your father and your mother, as the Lord your God has commanded you, that your days may be long, and that it may be well with you in the land which the Lord your God is giving you."
Deuteronomy 5:18

What should you do if your parents don't give their consent? Your best reaction will be to embark on serious prayer. As I said before, it is so important to get the blessing of your parents. So, if they are not supporting your relationship, seek to understnad why. They may raise some valid objections that you need to consider before committing yourself to marriage. Do not ignore their feelings, before giving due consideration to why your parents oppose your union.

Have fun in your courtship. It is a sad thing to see a couple get too serious too fast. At any stage of your relationship, refrain from being jealous and possessive or else you will cause endless contention in your courtship. It would be wise to put a relationship that is plagued with jealousy and possessiveness, on hold; at least temporarily until these issues are resolved. Consider this. God may have allowed you to become discontented because you either are going too far too quickly, or you are pursuing the wrong person. Any couple, no matter how well suited, will quarrel every now and then. however, ongoing unhappiness is *definitely not God's plan. "...no good thing will he withhold from them that walk uprightly" Psalm 84:11.* The Bible says, *"Thou wilt show me the path of life: in thy presence is fullness of joy; at thy right hand there are pleasures for evermore" Psalm 16:11.*

If the presence of God brings pleasure, do you think He would assign any of His children the rigorous task of being with a person whose very presence robs you of the joy of the Lord?

Harsh words, mood swings and attitudes can kill the bond in any relationship. Whereas healthy words serve to promote your relationship. So select what you say wisely, remembering that your aim is to make your fiancée your best friend.

TAKE

At this point, your relationship is ready for marriage; you've fallen in love and you're aware of each other's strengths and weaknesses. It takes a good man to love his wife the way God loves her, and it takes a good woman to respect, honour and submit to her husband. Your motivation to marry someone should be that you will help them to fulfill God's assignment for their lives, and that both of you make it in heaven. God has purposed that marriage be like a team, fulfilling His call for the lives of each person - together - while pleasing one another, but with a primary focus on Him - and not for simply satisfying your own personal desires. Marriage was ultimately designed to be a service to God.

SEIZE THE GRACE

Chapter 3

PRE-MARITAL COUNSELING

Pre-marital counseling is designed to teach couples the truth about marriage, according to the Bible. That is why it is very important to go for premarital counseling before you commit yourself to someone. when you are under church counsel, it will be much easier for you to go to your leaders for advice when you run into problems.

The Bible doesn't give any direction about pre-marital counseling. The closest I would think is when Paul spoke about the issue of marriage in 1 Corinthians 7. He acknowledged that it is better to marry than burn with lust; he warns us that marriage will bring challenges and pressures.

The majority of couples who seek expert counsel find that it increases the chances their marriages will last. Be open to counsel. The Bible says, 'Pride...breeds quarrels, but wisdom is found in those who take advice. Proverbs 13:10.

WONDERFUL WEDDINGS FOLLOWED BY MISERABLE MARRIAGES

Many couples spend more time preparing for the wedding than they do preparing for marriage. Consequently, these wonderful weddings end in miserable marriages.

Pre-marital counseling is important because, one day when you are in trouble, you will need help. One of the reasons there's so much divorce in the Christian circles is because some Christians never went for premarital counseling. They just want to jump on the wagon and go. They think they know everything. Some people go for pre-marital counseling and are warned of possible trouble, but still they take it lightly thinking they can beat the odds. They think being in love is so special that they would never quarrel or encounter trouble. But in the end, pursuing a marriage without heeding good counsel usually results in divorce.

Love alone can not sustain a marriage that was doomed from the start because it lacked guidance from knowing elders, and from God Himself. When seeking counsel approach it with a teachable spirit and you will indeed benefit from it. As your marriage prospers you will be glad that you made a wise choice.

Couples that marry without having premarital counseling are at much higher risk of divorce.

If you have been married previously and are planning to get married again, you will still need to undertake pre-marital counseling. Do not be over confident and think you know everything about marriage, because you have experienced it before. There is always room for improvement and adjustment. Counselling helps you to see potential problems that you previously missed, and will guide you to resolve them.

It is in your best interest to take on board the advice given to you by the counsellors and elders who have already been there and done it before you. They have wisdom and experience that you may lack, and have discovered secrets of having a happy marriage that you can benefit from. Even if you never had a chance to go for pre-marital counselling, you don't have to sit in your home with problems thinking it is too late to do anythinga about it. My advice is to see your pastor or seek out Christian counsellors. Remember that you don't have to figure out everything on your own.

Contrary to commonly held ideas, good marriages do not just happen. You need to seek Gods will, follow His instructions and you will see God come through for both of you. Even if you are church leaders who have general knowledge of the Bible, you will still need pre-marital counselling. Some churches do not require pre-marital counselling for church leaders because the leaders have a good understanding of Christianity; yet the divorce rate for Christians is about the same as for non-Christian marriages. Therefore I advise that everybody, irrespective of your position or title, seek out good pre-marital counsel.

Job said, "Let age speak". Allow these who have been there before you to minister to you, equip you, teach you and warn you of what is to come in the journey ahead, so that you can gain understanding about how to stand whenever you run into trouble. I don't expect that you will always be in trouble, yet inevitably you will have misunderstandings, so good counsel will help you when you need it. Be teachable and you will be reachable. Proverbs 11:14 advises that without counsel people fall but in the abundance of counsel there is safety.

"For when for the time ye ought to be teachers, ye have need that one teach you again which be the first principles of the oracles of God; and are become such as have need of milk, and not of strong meat" Hebrews 5:12.

You will not be able to teach effectively unless you

yourself are teachable. "Two heads are better than one." Ask for help. God is able to boost you when you stay teachable. Your pastors and Christian counsellors will correct you and show you what you will need.

Unfortunately, some Christians choose not to go to their pastors for counseling when they are in trouble, and later on you here news that they are divorced. Not everyone is willing to listen, and some get annoyed quickly; justifying themselves by saying "who are you to judge me."

When you are faced with problems in marriage and have never had any pre-marital counseling, the devil will easily lie to you and it will affect you more than those who had counseling. The devil will tell you that the easiest and most logical thing to do is to quit or to go to court. The devil is a trickster and cunning. He is a liar, and you can better stand against His guiles when you have been properly prepared through counselling.

Those who make themself unteachable face tough consequences. Don't be tempted to give up and leave your marriage prematurely. Napoleon hill commented that *"One of the most common causes of failure is the habit of quitting when one is overtaken by temporary defeat."* Always aim to learnearn from other people's mistakes so that you don't fall into the same pitfalls as others do. Failure can be turned into success when you learn from your mistakes.

Some people, when they go for help don't want to be corrected; instead they argue or resist until they get their own way. If you have an unteachable spirit, it will be difficult for the Holy Spirit to walk with you. The Holy Spirit is a teacher and He can only teach those who yield to Him. Study the following scriptures and see what they say about the importance of counsel:

"Whoso loveth instruction loveth knowledge: but he that hateth reproof is brutish." Proverbs 12:1

A scorner loveth not one that reproveth him: neither will he go unto the wise." Proverbs 15:12

Without counsel purposes are disappointed: but in the multitude of counselors they are established." Proverbs 15:22

Age should speak, and multitude of years should teach wisdom." Job 36:5

"A wise man will hear, and will increase learning; and a man of understanding shall attain unto wise counsels." Proverbs 1:5

I will now share with you a story of a wedding which had all the makings of a fairytale, yet ended tradically. The couple had just exchanged vows in a romantic Castle that featured in a TV show. But things soon turned sour when the bride was arrested at the reception after attacking her husband and trashing a hotel room. The new bride spent a weekend in the cells after hitting the groom on the head with her stiletto shoe in a row, while guests partied downstairs. The staff in the hotel had to call the police after the groom appeared at reception clutching a bloodstained towel. The police found the groom sitting on the bed in a hotel room, strewn with broken glass? A broken lamp was on the floor and wires had been pulled out of sockets, causing about £500 worth of damage. Instead of enjoying their honeymoon, the day ended in total chaos. The newly wed wife told the police she and her husband had 'both been accusing each other of different things' and she had hit him on the head only because he took hold of her. The wife admitted assaulting her husband and damaging the room. She was fined for damaging the room and ordered to pay the hotel £500 in compensation. By the grace of God they forgave each other and are living together. But what an aweful way to start your marriage! I believe this couple never had time to go for counseling, otherwise they may have avoided this outcome. We can avoid a lot of chaos if we humble ourselves, be taught and take direction as the Bible commands us.

As divorce rates are rocketing, nations, communities and governments find themselves in serious trouble. The importance of pre-marital counselling cannot be overstated. Whenever I hear of marriages breaking down, I often wonder if they courted for a healthy length of time, and if they took pre-marital counseling. I feel strength that because people are not properly prepared for marriage when there first storm arrives, they pack it in and call it quits. Without a doubt, you can not fail an exam you studied for! By this I mean a marriage can not fail if you put in the right ingredients to begin with and then grow in the right direction. It is advisable to wait patiently for marriage. Wait patiently for your time to get into marriage. There is no need to rush. If that man or woman is yours, no one can take them from you. Did you know that grasshoppers know when to migrate? They can never migrate before their season; or after their season so you too must wait patiently for your season.

"Yea, the stork in the heaven knows her appointed times; and the turtle and the crane and the swallow observe the time of their coming; but my people know not the judgment of the LORD." Jeremiah 8:7

This means that in God's right time you will marry or get married (2 Peter 3:8). God works to His own timing and often it is completely different from ours. God promises to make all things work out for our good, in His time. Resist

"RUSHING THE INGREDIENTS OF A RECIPE MAKES A BAD CUISINE"
-ANONYMOUS-

the temptation to run ahead of God's divine calendar. It is always in your best interest to wait. They that wait upon the Lord He will renew their strength they shall run and not grow weary (Isaiah 40:31). God's divine timing is always best. When your relatinoship progresses in line with God's divine timing, you avoid pressure and frustration which marks many hurried relationships. It it advisable to seek the Lord by waiting on Him through fasting and prayer concerning when to enter marriage; for they that seek the Lord understand all things (Proverbs 18:5).

Before you seek to enter marriage, you must first come to a place of mental maturity. A mature character is not necessarily the product of age, but rather a fruit of spiritual growth. When considering pre-marital counselling, seek out mature, experienced leaders to counsel you. During the course of counselling, marriage is well defined and carefully observed.

Because a couple are made accountable for their actions, the risk of abuse occuring in marriage is reduced. Mature counsellors will provide a rich store of knowledge that will help you to stand when storms come because you have been groomed and prepared for when challenges come. You need mentors not only in your life, ministry, and business but also in your marriage, so that you can get good counsel and direction, and the necessary assistance to blossom in your union. Who do you speak to when you're in a storm? You should be speaking to mentors who are experienced and have survived the test that you are passing through. Seek God and find out what His will is for your life, allowing Him to guide you in all your endeavours.

Pre-marital counseling will teach you what to expect in marriageso that no situation will take you by surprise and you will learn how to fulfil your marital duties. Many long standing traditions within the family have changed during the 21st century. Husbands are no longer the sole breadwinner, with women now being economically active, and contributing to the family income.

"For by wise counsel you shall make your war: and in multitude of counselors there is safety." Proverbs 24:6

Your pastor or a Christian counsellor will advise you not to have sex before marriage. If you go against this advice, you may find that on your honeymoon you will run out of activities to do and may even get bored because you had already engaged in pre-marital sex. Whereas, those who don't have sex prior to marriage will hardly leave their room because they are having fun and are very excited. They say that marriage kills sex, but I agree with a comment I once heard, "It is not marriage that kills sex, but pre-marital sex kills marriage."

Planning for the wedding is also another crucial point that will be looked at during the course of your counselling. You will be advised to make sure that all legal requirements are met, i.e. a letter of consent from the parents, licenses, blood tests, etc (we will look at this at blood testing at end of this chapter).

Other important issues that will be addressed by pre-marital counselling, like when your ministries are not compatible.

For example, if one partner is training to be a foreign missionary and the other is a pastor of a local church, then it is likely that one of the two will have to give up his or her dreams for the success of the other, because they can not make both dreams come true and live together happily at the same time. If both of you are church leaders, and one is an intercessor, while the other preaches, then it is fair to say that your visions are compatible. Counselling also teaches the important skill of evaluating your relationship by way of assessing its strengths and weaknesses. You also benefit from learning how to communicate effectively, and gain tools for dealing with marital conflicts. This often involves reviews some deadly patterns that kill relatinships, such as personal differences and how they impact upon your relationship is also addressed.

SEMINARS AND CONFERENCE

I encourage you, every now and then to attend seminars, workshops on marriage. Buy tapes and CD's of well respected men and women of God who have been through the process of marriage before you. It will help you to improve on your marriage skills. Solomon asked for knowledge and wisdom and God was pleased with him not only did He give him what he requested but He gave him riches along with it (2 Chronicles 1: 10-12).

It will also help you to continue attending seminars and conferences about marriage and the family, once married. You can gain a wealth of wisdom and understanding from these teachings. Men, do not let your ego get in the way of an opportunity to learn and grow - attend these meetings also all too often women take advantage of such events, while their husbands pass up the opportunity. This can result in wives becoming more wise and knowledgeable than their husbands.

There are women and men of God who He has anointed to impart rgace into the marriages of those whose marriages need reviving.

I attend marriage conferences with my husband and we have been truly blessed by the things we've learnt. Through these conference our love for one another has been rekindled. I have learnt how to treat my husband and He has learnt how to treat me. We have been challenged, and we have grown as a result. Peter and I admire couples of God who love each other and purpose in our hearts that we will follow their good examples.

My husband and I have been in marriage for twenty years but even now we are still learning and growing with each other. When you learn new skills to build your marriage, put it into practice. Be doers of God's word. It will benefit your relationship to use new tactics that you have learnt, if they help to enrich your marriage.

"But be doers of the word, and not hearers only, deceiving yourselves. For if anyone is a hearer of the word and not a doer, he is like a man observing his natural face in a mirror; for he observes himself, goes away, and immediately forgets what kind of man he was. But he who looks into the perfect law of liberty and continues in it, and is not a forgetful hearer but a doer of the work, this one will be blessed in what he does." James 1:22-25

SEXUAL TESTING

Testing for sexual diseases is also a topic addressed by pre-marital counselling. It is so crucial, yet some couples are afraid of it through fear that they may lose their prospective spouse. The reality is that some people would rather avoid anything that they feel might hinder them from attaining the marriage status.

In our pre-marital counseling sessions, ladies reveal that they would want to have an HIV test but find it difficult suggesting it to their partners. This is very common in African settings. This is because of the subordinate position of women within those societies; and the fear some women have of being accused of promiscuity, or for not trusting their partners.

HIV testing before marriage is advisable as a negative test results will help the couple stay safe within their marriage; those who find out that they are positive and decide to go ahead and get wed can access treatments and preventive services such as condoms, prevention of mother-to-child transmission of the virus, and other drugs and remedies.

HIV counseling and testing should be compulsory for couples intending to get married, including customary marriages. As I mentioned before, we need a law or guidelines to support such implementation of these tests.

Young women are particularly vulnerable; they are four times as likely to be infected as their male counterparts. This is because over half of African women marry while still in their teens; yet they get married to older men who may have had many sexual partners before. Some of these men may have acquired HIV or other Sexually Transmitted Infections (STI's) that they transmit to their young wife.

As you can see, pre-marital counselling covers a wide

range is issues that are relevant to a couple that plan to get married and spend their lives together. Its benefits are immense, and it provides great support and direction to couples early in their relationship journey.

Chapter 4

HONEYMOON

"When a man has taken a new wife, he shall not go out to war or be charged with any business; he shall be free at home one year, and bring happiness to his wife whom he has taken." Deuteronomy 24:5

I want to use this scripture to support the issues of having a honeymoon. In this case the bride and bridegroom were given a long period of time to be away. Deuteronomy provides wisdom we can learn from, and demonstrates the importance of a new couple spending quality time with each other, soon after getting wed. The aim is to make their affection for each other grow. According to this scripture, if the husband was to stay long abroad the first year, his love for his wife would be in danger of growing cold, or opportunity may arise for him to be drawn to other women he might meet while he's abroad, or away somewhere for a prolonged period of time.

In Deuteronomy we see that neither military service nor business responsibilities were to take a man away from his wife during the first year of marriage. Instead, he was to remain home and "bring happiness" to his wife. Studies show the importance of the first months of marriage in acquainting newly weds and establishing marital patterns. Attending to marriage as a high priority helps to ensure its success.

The honeymoon period is godly and biblical. During this time you need to work on developing your romance; the honeymoon is a time for seclusion and erotic warmth. It is time a for both of you to keep away from the family and friends so that you may maximise this quality time together. Very few couples give the honeymoon much thought. Yet the honeymoon will be essential in setting the tone for life as a married couple. It will help you make the new and more intimate adjustments to each other that marriage requires.

When planning for your honeymoon, pick a perfect place to pamper your beloved, and delight in each moment of passion. If your budget will afford, romantic places like Paris are interesting places to explore. Paris is said to be the world's capital of love and romance - a kiss here, another there! You can explore the magnificent hotels and tourist resorts, and seek advice from a tour and travel agency. They are able to tailor a package to suit your budget and requirements so that you can make the most of your honeymoon. Depending on your taste, you can adventure to romantic getaways and indulge in fun sports that are on offer, like surfing and the like.

When Peter and I had our honey moon, it was not too long and not too short. We did not want to overspend. It's not advisable to start a marriage that way. To avoid financial difficulties, when planning a honeymoon trip, you should keep in mind that you are beginning a long journey through life together. It is good to form a budget at the outset. In our case we also thought being away for long be come boring. I have known couples to come back home only to wish that they had not invested in such an expensive wedding trip, before embarking on the road of life together, be wise and plan ahead.

If you have financial difficulties, don't feel obliged to have an extravagant honeymoon. You may postpone the honeymoon to a time when you are better able to afford it. If you delay your wedding, make sure you have adequate privacy, it is not time to invite your family members to live with you or visit. If you previously had relatives stay with you who are under your care, plan another place for them so that you don't start straining your marriage.

When you finally consumate your marriage, engage in your love-making with sensitivity. Ensure that you are considerate of each other during sex. Beoming sexually adjusted to one another can take time and will require patience. By being gentle and considerate you can avoid shattering the happiness of the honeymoon and the marriage itself. This is yet another reason why pre-marital counselling is so importnat; it addresses these issues so you are prepared when you encounter them. We shall look at this topic of sex in details later on in the book.

YOUR NEW HOME

Whatever you do, plan your home arrangements together, and consult each other for ideas and advice. Wives often have the best ideas for how arrangements for the home should be, but husbands should not be excluded from making contribution - after all, it is a shared home, so his involvement is valuable. Make plans and finalise your living arrangements, in advance of your wedding.

If you have relatives and friends you trust, ask them to support you with your wedding plans; you will appreciate the help you get, as some people find wedding planning stressful. Ideally, the husband should organise the marital home for the comfort of his wife. I don't believe in a man marrying someone's daughter and taking her to live at his parent's home. No! If you are not ready to rent a room or a house, then wait until you are ready before stepping into marriage; otherwise you run the risk of starting your marriage with problems from in-laws. And this is not the wisest way to begin your marriage.

In the initial stages of setting up your marital home display your wedding pictures, in celebration of your union. Open your wedding presents together, this will be a moment to cherish later on. I share many ideas on how to decorate your house in my book *"Woman you are Great."*

BACK TO WORK

Everything has a beginning and an end and unfortunately honeymoons don't last forever. During your honeymoon you would have been going to bed late, waking up late, visiting places and spending money. The honeymoon allows you to spend a lot of time together, but eventually this privilege will have to change, to some extent or other. when you return to your normal routine you may find some things overwhelming, like going back to work. So be prepared!

When my husband and I give pre- marital counselling to couples, we advise them to plan their annual leave way in advance, to cooincide with the first wedding anniversary. This provides the perfect opportunity for you to go back and reflect on your romantic honeymoon, and to cherish your union. We all need such times to build our relationship bond. Some ministers of the gospel make themselves so busy and they leave their own marriages to suffer. This is not a healthy balance and I advise you not to follow suite.

At times when you are away from your partner, call them every so often and let them know you are thinking of them. But don't over do it. You need to catch up on the pile of work in the office or your business also. Don't be shocked when your colleagues make jokes about your new status, it is part of life, simply enjoy the fun. Put your partner's photo on your desk. Let everybody know that you're newly married. Be mindful not to let your coworkers feel neglected. Although uyour spouse will become priority, continue to invest time with your colleagues, going out to lunch together and engaging them in conversatin, as you did before.

Whatever you do be wise in your dealings with your colleagues, sitting next to each other at work doesn't necessarily lead to temptation, but if two people get along well, spending all day together can certainly nurture a connection. Don't be jealous of all your partner's co-workers, instead note if your spouse seems to be spending all their time with one co-worker in particular or talking to and about a particular colleague. If you notice such a pattern then you may have a valid reason to uncomfortable with the situation.

Even in an educational setting you may need to exercise caution in relation to how your spouse interacts with others. you may want to discuss and gree some boundaries with your partner; so that you both feel conortable with how each other relates to felow student and lecturers; as you would for coworkers.

The honeymoon is intended to strengthen the bond in a relationship and to unite you more closely, and in an intimate way. Therefore, make the most of it while it lasts, and remember that it is a foundational time for your marriage.

Chapter 5

MARRIAGE COVENANT

The only Scripture in the Bible where you actually find the word 'covenant' used in direct relationship to marriage is in Malachi.

"Because the Lord has been a witness between you and the wife of your youth, against whom you have dealt treacherously, though she is your companion and your wife by covenant." Malachi 2:14

So here we see how the Lord refuses to bless a man because his wife is being mistreated in some form. However, Malachi points out that the man's attitude towards his wife is only an indicator of a much deeper problem. Husbands if you mistreat your wives your prayers are hindered. Wives must also take care to honour and respect their husbands (1 Peter 3:7).

Covenant as defined by the scriptures is a solemn and binding relationship which is meant to last a life time. It has been said, "A covenant expresses a relationship which God Himself sovereignly initiates out of His own choice and decision." It is important to understand that a covenant brings oneness between covenant partners. When you know this truth, it will set you free (John 8:36), free to live as we should in our marriages, and not to live as we please.

When you sleep with someone and engage in sexual intercourse, there is a blood exchange. It means you have made a covenant with that person. Anytime there's sex between a man and a woman, they are making a statement that they are married. I have heard many questions asked in our marriage conference regarding this issue. They ask, "Does it mean that since we have had sex we don't need to go to church after all we are married through having sex?" I always tell them that it's not right because they have not honored God who ordained marriage, they are in fornication. They have not also honored their parents; therefore there are no blessings from both God and the parents.

As I made clear, if you get into an intimate relationship with someone, you have by doing so made a 'covenant' with that person. There will develop what is known as a soul tie; your spirit will be open to that person. Any union of this kind will mean you become one with whom you have sex with, both in body and in spirit.

This will affect your relationship with God. And if the person is already married, the relationship with their husband or wife suffers too. If their spouse becomes aware of your wrongdoing they might want to divorce. Be warned however! If you get wrongly involved with someone's partner, their covenant stands against you; and there will be serious consequences for your sin. Some people have lost pregnancies, even when they finally settle in marriage. Others suffer broken marriages, because they opened themselves up to the demonic world by interferring with someone else's covenant. Other consequences include the inability to enjoy sex. In case you find yourself in such a position, go to your pastor and ask him or her to lead you in prayers of deliverance.

Sex out of marriage will bring a curse and destruction. This glorifies the devil and the godly marriage glorifies God. Yet, if you have fallen into fornication, all is not over. You can repent, receive God's forgiveness and live a pure life, according to God's word.

Guilt has been known to become a block to sexual enjoyment, and can cause orgasmic malfunction in marriages. Many marriages are facing this problem, yet those involved find it difficult to talk about it.

Unfortunately for some, marriage has become a little more than an upgraded social contract between two people, rather than a lifetime holy covenant between two partners and their God. In the Old Testament days, a covenant was solemn and binding. When two people entered into a covenant with one another, a goat or lamb would be slain and its carcass would be cut in half. With the two halves separated and lying on the ground, the couple who formed the covenant would solemnize their promise by walking between the two halves saying, "May God do so to me (cut me in half) if I ever break this covenant with you and God!" You get the feeling that a covenant in those days had just a little more substance than today.

I noticed that the Bible opens and closes with scenes of the marriage. The first marriage is between Adam and Eve. The last marriage is between Christ and His Bride. And these two marriage scenes tell the story of redemption. And so we have a Bible that wraps itself around the institution of marriage.

Marriage is God's design – 'One man for one woman' as we read in Genesis, the book of beginnings...

In the beginning God created the heavens and the earth…(1:26) Then God said, "Let Us make man in

Our image, according to Our likeness …(2:18) Then the LORD God said, "It is not good for the man to be alone; I will make him a helper, who is suitable, adapted and complementary for him" (1:1).

Although the word "covenant" is not actually used, Moses describes what the union represents in essence; it was the first "covenant of marriage."

The bible tells that the Lord God caused a deep sleep to fall upon the man, and he slept. Then He took out one of his ribs and closed up the flesh. And the LORD God fashioned into a woman the rib which He had taken from the man and brought her to the man. And the man said, "This is now bone of my bones and flesh of my flesh." She shall be called Woman, because she was taken out of man. *"For this cause a man shall leave his father and his mother, and shall cleave to his wife and they shall become one flesh." Genesis 2:2-24*

Let me draw your attention to a pertinent statement from this scripture, "they shall become one flesh," it pictures the essence of covenant. Yes, marriage is a covenant, and much more. Biblical marriage is a divine picture of Christ and His Bride. In addition to that, biblical marriage speaks to us of the mystery of Deity.

In the marriage the wife can be likened to the Holy Spirit, and the man to the Word of God. It takes the harmonious union of both to produce life.

Marriage is the most sacred of covenants. In fact the Hebrew words for "marriage" and "holiness" is the same; kiddushin. Marriage is the only covenant in the Bible that allows two people to be perfectly joined in all areas of life, from the physical to the spiritual.

At the time of writing this book, I am old enough to testify of the profound impact that the concept of a covenamt had on Christian marriage. In 1995, a twenty-five year old marriage came into serious trouble. Both had been born again about 10 years earlier. In the sovereignty of God, a Precept Ministries inductive Bible study about covenants was offered at their local church, during the day and in the evening, which allowed the couple to attend. The Spirit of God worked with the biblical truth on covenant and radically transformed the troubled marriage, restoring the "years that the locusts had eaten." What transpired was nothing short of a miracle! What a testimony! Although, I cannot promise you a miracle, if your marriage is in need of an infusion of transforming grace, it might just be that you need to understand the significance of covenant in relation to marriage. God's Spirit can open your eyes to understand covenant and through it, it can revitalize, revive or restore your relationship.

When you experience challenges in marriage, don't give up because things may look bad even if storms are hitting you left, right and centre. Remember that no storm lasts forever. This does mean you should stay in a physically abusive marriage, where your life is at risk - no! People may misunderstand you, talk about you, laugh at you, alienate you, not invite you over, refuse to support you; but you can make it on your own, with God as your strength. He will see you through your marital trials. Your God is a covenant making, covenant keeping God, and what He has spoken over your life He will surely bring to pass; no matter what situations you may walk through in life. Depend on Him, He keeps His word (Romans 3:4).

"ONE OF THE MOST COMMON CAUSES OF FAILURE IS THE HABIT OF QUITTING WHEN ONE IS OVERTAKEN BY TEMPORARY DEFEAT."
-NAPOLEON HILL-

Marriage is like a garden, it requires maintenance. To stay at its best it needs to be prepared and cultivated, constantly; just the same as a good marriage. The reason there may be weeds growing instead of roses in your garden is because you spend enough time planting rose seeds. Listen friend! Your marriage is not just a covenant before God; it's a shelter for your passions and dysfunction. You honor God by treating your marriage as precious. Now that you have understood that marriage is a covenant you made before God, realise that you can't just simply break it. If God considers the breaking of a human covenant a very serious matter and one which will bring judgment on the guilty party, how much more the covenant we make with Him when entering marriage? God Himself established the covenant of marriage, for this reason marriage thrives on Him, as we are going to see in the following next chapter.

Chapter 6

MARRIAGE THRIVES ON GOD

"And a threefold cord is not quickly broken."
Ecclesiastes 4:12b

Here we see in this scripture that a threefold cord is not quickly broken. This means that because you are closely joined in holy love and fellowship, God will be with you, strengthening your tie, so that your love will not be easily broken. It is possible to live together with your partner and live together in unity. Opposition will undoubtedly come but because the Most High is between you, He will help you fight your battles, if you allow Him to be an integral part of your union. Look at the God head in heaven. God the Father, the Son and the Holy Spirit live together in perfect harmony and in power. They do not compete or strive with one another. They are a threefold cord which cannot be broken.

After settling into the marriage routine, some couples may find themselves thinking and saying words they never expected to say; and conducting themselves in ways that are not conducive to building a fruitful marriage.

For example:

"I'm leaving. This isn't the person I thought I was marrying. Life is too short for all of this pain. We're no longer good for one another."

"We've tried everything. Nothing seems to work. She just insists on having everything her own way. It's useless. The only thing to do is bail out."

"Look at how high the divorce rate is. Everybody's getting a divorce - even prominent church leaders. So why should I suffer through a bad marriage? There's no need for me to be the exception."

"Our marriage needs a little excitement. We're too used to each other. Maybe if I have an affair, it will put the spice back into our marriage."

"We've been going from counselor to counselor. I don't know how much money we've spent. We even

went to a preacher. Somebody must have the right formula for us. I guess we'll just have to keep searching."

"I guess I'm destined to a life of unhappiness. There's nothing I can do about my marriage. Maybe when the children all leave home I'll have the courage to get out. Until then, I'll just have to pretend everything's okay."

Your marriage thrives and depends on God. As we explained earlier, He is the one who initiated marriage right from the beginning; and He has all the answers. So why would you keep Him out of your life and marriage? Develop a routine of asking for more grace everyday. It works my friend. I have experienced God giving me His Grace everyday, when I ask him for it. Don't allow the devil to preach to and sow his negative perspective into your mind. Go back to God in prayer when you encounter chalenging time in your relationship. It was God who got you into your marriage, and it will be Him who gets you through the tough times. He is the one who blessed you with your family.

I remember when Peter and I had problems in our marriage, the Holy Spirit revealed to us that our relationship with Him was declining and we had allowed other things to take the time we should have devoted to God. We were busy with church, work and our family. The statements listed above was a erality for us, we considered the idea that our marriage was not working out, and that we should seperate.

Our predicament revealed to us that the quality of our marriage life is greatly affected by the time we spend with God, and therefore we should never swap God's time for anything else, no matter how appealing an alternative might seem. God is always a priority. The more time you spend in His presence the less time you will spend quarrelling with yuor spouse. Your arguing will be replaced by peace. As you experience God's presence you will begin to see such a big change in your life and your marriage. Your partner will also see a change in you; and it will be easier for you to get along with each other, as God's presence will give you the grace to live together harmoniously.

The things you once found hard will become easier as you live daily in His presence. You will becom more temperate and increasingly more sensitive to God's Spirit. When He speaks to you about being calm and patient with your spouses. The grace of God will provide the grace for you to grow in the fruit of the

Spirit. You will find it easier to say sorry to your partner if you cause offence. One of the benefits of my intimate relationship with God is that the Holy Spirit always warns me when I am going to fall out with my husband. He will whisper to me, "be quiet, danger is on the way." When I listen, I see good results but when I don't, I get into hot soup. I have seen the good results of obeying the Holy Spirit. Never be too busy to spend time with your God; you need His grace. When you are willing to make adjustments to your lifestyle to factor in more time for God, your marriage will become enriched with happiness.

THE COMFORTER

God has given us someone who is always there for us; the Holy Spirit; He will comfort you. Practice going before God and allowing Hs Spirit to confort you.
"Blessed be the God and Father of our Lord Jesus Christ, the Father of mercies and God of all comfort, who comforts us in all our tribulation that we may be able to comfort those who are in any trouble, with the comfort with which we ourselves are comforted by God." 2 Corinthians 1:3-4

Many times when we have misunderstandings, we are often quick to go to friends. This grieves the Holy

Spirit deeply because we fail to acknowledge Him and instead lean on the arm of flesh, which achieve little by companion. It is my routine to go before God in prayer and to read His word. I confess it out loud to myself and through His word, I experience the power of His presence.

The beauty of God's word is that it has the power to encourage and comfort you. The Holy Spirit is the best comforter; He is my personal source of comfort; not my husband. Of course Peter tries to comfort me when I am down, but he is limited in what he can do. The Holy Spirit is the best comforter there is - only He is able to minister to the deep hidden places of your heart. That is why nurturing a good relationship with Him is so important, because if you fall out with your spouse you always have someone to turn to. His arms are outstretched towards you always. Even when you ignore Him for sometime, He is waiting for you to repent and return to Him. At any time He is able and willing to support and strengthen your relationship. He is the source you can draw on anytime; you will profit everytime you let Him guide you concerning your decision making in every area of your life, including your marriage.

So when you find yourself in a struggle remember that seperating is not the only option. Although divorce is permissible under some circumstances - in the case of adultery and abuse; it is not a decision that should ever be taken lightly. God makes clear His position on divorce in Malachi 2:16, *"For the Lord God of Israel says That He hates divorce, For it covers one's garment with violence," Says the Lord of hosts. "Therefore take heed to your spirit that you do not deal treacherously."*

"Happy is he who has the God of Jacob for his help, whose hope is in the Lord his God..." Psalms 146:5

When you seek help from God in the middle of a marital crisis, and even when you are happy, God will give you new joy because you have made Him your help and support. Place your hope in him; He that trusts in God is happy! When you are facing challenges in your marriage or at your place of work, the Lord will reach down from on high and rescue your marriage - but you must trust Him. As long as you have the right motives, you can always call on Him. As long as you're not calling Him to kill your partner, in-laws, or boss, as some people are sometimes misguided to do - shocking but true!

"We don't wrestle against flesh and blood but against principalities, against powers, against the rulers of the darkness of this age, against spiritual hosts of

wickedness in the heavenly places." Ephesians 6:12.

"The Lord is near to all who call upon Him, to all who call upon Him in truth." Psalms 145:18

The Lord continually searches our hearts and examines our minds. That is why you should sure you clear your mind, of all ill-motives, and ask God purge your heart; so that you will get rid your life of bitterness and revenge. If you do not your prayers may not be answered. What you need are results. Forget about revenge. As the saying goes, "Before you embark on a journey of revenge, dig two graves." Get rid of revenge. Uzziah sought God in the days of Zechariah, who had understanding in the visions of God; and as long as he sought the Lord, God made him prosper (2 Chronicles 26:5). Do you want to prosper in your marriage? Then learn how to seek the God of success.

The word seek comes from the Hebrew word *'darash'*. It means to ask, especially to worship, care diligently, inquire, usually to follow (for pursuit or search). So Uzziah worshipped God with all His heart. He diligently inquired of the Lord before he ventured into anything. That is what God expects you to do. Worship Him in spirit and in truth. You should teach your children to worship God, and He will make them prosper in whatever they do. Prosper in this verse comes from a Hebrew word 'tsalach' meaning break out, go over, go forward. As long as Uzziah sought the Lord, he progressed in life; the same principle applies to you.

Do you want to go forward in your marriage? Then my advice is to seek God as long as you live. Diligently inquire of Him in whatever you do, be it leading your family, raising your children? Rely on God! Your marriage cannot thrive without the Almighty God, Creator of the universe. It is by His Grace that Peter and I enjoy our marriage; and it will be by His grace that you will enjoy yours.

A plant can't thrive, or blossom if it becomes disconnected from its roots it will die. And the same rules apply to us. If we keep God out of our lives, we will not succeed in our marriage. Our life will be plagued with failure and we will die miserable and unfulfilled. When a car breaks down, you take it to the garage for repair. The garage may contact the manufacturer, if the missing part is out of stock. The same should happen with our marriages. Go back to God; let Him be in the centre of your marriage; and allow him to orchestrate the repair of any damages caused. No demon, no evil spirit will be able to fight you and prevail, against you marriage, whan you submit your life to Christ and trust in Him for your solutions.

Pray and ask the Lord to give you new mercies in your marriage, everyday (Lamentations 3:23). Without His mercies, you will not be able to manage the pressures that often come in marriage.

God promised the children of Israel, fresh manna each day but some went ahead to gather more than they needed for the day. Moses warned them not to save any of it but they didn't listen; and so the extra manner they gathered bred worms and became foul. The same happens to us when we pray today and we don't pray the next day, thinking that yesterday's prayers will sustain. Or we read the word today and we think we don't need to read it tomorrow, since we read His word yesterday. The word you read and the prayer you prayed yesterday was not meant to take you through the week. Prayer and reading God's word should become a daily activity, so that you receive new mercies, fresh revelations, and fresh anointing in your marriage day by day.

"...pray without ceasing; in everything give thanks; for this is the will of God in Christ Jesus for you. 1 Thessalonians 5:17

BE CONSISTENT

Jesus shared a parable with his disciples telling them to consistently pray without giving up (Luke 18:1). If you are to receive answers for your prayers, you must be consistent. Stand firm in your faith, pray for your spouse earnestly and fervently, then wait patiently for change. For you to thrive everyday in your union, pray that the glory of the Lord will be revealed in your marriage, because when the unmarried see God's glory in your marriage, they will be encouraged to get married and to stand when marriage tornadoes and storms come their way. A friend of mine one day told me that when she sees the way my husband and I handle each other, given what we have gone through, she is inspired to remain loyal to her husband. It's not easy to pray and wait but it's worth the effort. Praying can be difficult because our enemy, the devil, will do anything to discourage us from praying. He lies to us. He has done it to me and will lie to you too. He'll tell you that 'God is not interested in your prayers, that's why you have not seen any results.' If you are not careful, you can end up believing him, and failing to pray when you most need it.

I pray this will never be your portion in Jesus' name. Never underestimate the power of prayer. It is imperative for your marriage to keep on triving, and for others to see the glory of God in Christian relationships.

"Therefore I say to you, whatever things you ask when you pray, believe that you receive them, and you will have them." Mark 11:24

When you pray for your marriage, believe God to change your spouse with time. I have seen God changing my husband through prayer. There are times when I discern that the decision he is about to make is wrong. If I try to advice and he doesn't listen, I don't make it a big deal. I go on my knees in prayer and before I know it, he has reversed the decision.

Even if you are unsure of how to pray for your spouse, God is so caring that He has given us the Holy Spirit to teach us and help us to pray effectively. Ask Him to help you!

"The Spirit also helps our weaknesses, for we don't know how to pray as we ought. But the Spirit himself makes intercession for us with groaning which can't be uttered." Romans 8:26

By the help of the Holy Spirit, you can pray. And the

good news is when you do, your situation is going to change. Stop calling people and telling them your problems! Rather, go to God in prayer. Your friends can't change your spouse; they can't change your kid who is going wayward. Only the Almighty God can; He is bigger than your problem, your problem is never too big for Him to solve. In order for our marriages to run smoothly, they need servicing from God, and on a daily basis, lest they lose that flavor of God's love, the anointing of God and the joy of your first romance. Finally, when you pray, believe that God has answered.

SEEKING GOD INDIVIDUALLY

"Immediately Jesus made His disciples get into the boat and go before Him to the other side, while He sent the multitudes away. And when He had sent the multitudes away, He went up on the mountain by Himself to pray." Matthew 14:22 – 23

Spending time with God alone is crucial in our lives. It is good to pray as a couple, but you should always have quiet time with God alone. Discipline yourself, whether your partner is around or not, so that even if your spouse is not around, you can still have fellowship with your God independently. Jesus had fellowship alone with His Father. It is not bad to be alone with God. There are times when it's absolutely necessary if one is to hear from God.

Many were the times when Jesus withdrew to lonely places and prayed (Luke 5:16).

He withdrew by boat privately to a (Matthew 14:13) and went up on a mountainside by Himself to pray.

When He was alone, the twelve...asked Him about the parables (Mark 4:10).

In the Old Testament Jacob was left alone, and a man wrestled with him till daybreak (Genesis 32:24). How about Jeremiah? He sat alone because God's hand was on him' (Jeremiah 15:17). I once heard a man of God say, "Your greatest spiritual victories come from the battles God calls you to fight when you're alone. Most times He outlines and clarifies His plans for your life when there's nobody else around. That's because He wants you to be more influenced by Him, than them!" I believe this is true.

When God's grooming you for a special work you'll be required to spend time outside the company of others. In Exodus God said, *'Moses alone is to approach...the people may not come up with him'* Exodus 24:2. God does not want you to be lonely, no! He wants you to be with Him so that you can glean all you can from Him. How about Daniel? He was left alone, gazing at this great vision' (Daniel 10:8).

If you wish to enjoy a successful marriage, it is critical that you always spare time for God. Fight any distractions, but make sure you spend quality time with the lover of your soul. He should be number one in your life. God always wants the first place in your life. Love Him above everything else. He is your most important partner, therefore, don't give Him the leftovers of your time; rather, you should bring Him the best, the first fruit. Cain failed to give God his best and God was not pleased. Genesis documents that Cain brought some fruits as an offering; was that a bad thing? No. Yet, unlike his brother Abel, who gave God the first fruit of his increase,Cain failed to offer God his best. Abel did well in offfering God fat portions from some of the first born of his flock (Genesis 4:2-5). We ought to follow the example of Abel and give our God the first fruits of our time.

When you give God your first fruit, He will multiply your offering back to you. Every time you pay your tithes, you make a statement that God is first place in your finances. Why would He not provide for a household that puts him first? Even when financial problems come, somehow God will see you through.

He will give you financial wisdom and strategy to turn your finances around for the better. In addition to money, you should also tithe your time to God. On any day, you should set time aside to spend with God, both as a couple and on your own. It is important that you talk to God personally each day. Remove all distractions, switch off your phone, read the word and pray. God will lead you through the day, and make it fruitful - when you walk and talk with Him.

Tithe your time as an act of faith. God registers your acts of faith and the sacrifice that you make. It's not your money or time He needs. He owns everything, so you can't impress him. What does impress Him is your obedience. Your heart impresses Him, when it is right and contrite. A good example from the Bible is the widow who gave her last two mites, while others others gave out of their abundance. The lady who offered her last two mites impressed Jesus because of the motive of her heart. Mathew 12:42-44.

You must be a prayerful person. Prayer supports marriage and strengthens marriage partners. Prayer and fellowship with the Holy Spirit should be our first priority. I have disciplined myself to go to bed early because I am an early riser. I wake up around 4:00a.m to pray, read the word of God, meditate on it and make sure I memorise some scriptures. This approach has helped me a lot, especially as a mother. I have noticed that if I did not wake up that early, there is no way I would have time to pray and have fellowship with my God because I need to attend to my little ones. When fellowshipping with God I would suggest that you find time that suits your situation. It might be before you go to bed, or any other time that fits in best with your lifestyle. I prefer to pray early in the morning as almost everybody is sleeping, which means there are no interruptions and my mind is clear.

If you notice weaknesses in your spouse, when you're alone, pray against those weaknesses and thank God for their strengths. This is also why it is important to pray alone. You have the the freedom to pour out your heart to God without any distractions. In your prayer time, pray for your children, your businesses, and ministry, as the Lord leads you.

If you are a single sister, pray that God will give you the grace to stand in times of trials. Pray for your future partner that God will keep them holy and use them for the glory of His name.

As a said before as a couple, remember you still have to know God individually. We have an example of

David in the Bible and how he knew God in his life.
When David returned home after returning the Ark of
the Covenant, he met his wife Michal, daughter of Saul
who came out to meet him. David knew God
personally. He loved God even above his wives. He
had caught a revelation of who God is. He also had a
good understanding of where God brought him from,
having graduated from shepherd boy to king. His
answer to her therefore was: "It was before the Lord,
who chose me rather than your father or anyone from
his house when he appointed me ruler over the Lord's
people Israel. I will celebrate before the Lord, I will
become even more undignified than this, and I will be
humiliated in my own eyes. But by these slave girls you
spoke of I will be held in honor." What an answer?
She was shocked! What a shame?

You have to know God individually; a person, even a
spouse can drive you away from your God. I have seen
the devil using husbands or wives to draw their
spouses away from God. And some don't do it
deliberately. A spouse can unintentionally discourage
you from serving God or praying, etc. Every time your
partner knows that you are going to do something for
God he or she may bring up a plan to take the whole
family away. Or when they know you are giving money
towards the work of God they may discourage you. So

what do you do in such a case? Ask God to give you wisdom. There are times when you have to compromise. God sees your heart. In other cases, you will have to go ahead and do what God says, i.e. tithing go ahead and tithe even if your spouse disagree with it. God must be first in your life. David chose to honor God first; he was not willing to compromise.

How about Abigail in the Bible? (1 Samuel 25: 16-18). She refused to compromise, she feared God more than her husband. I am not suggesting you rebel against your spouse. I don't mean you start leaving your spouse out of your plans - no! Rather, ask God to give you wisdom concerning difficult cases. So that have the grace to deal with situations in the most effective way.

King Ahab failed to fear, honor, and put God first in his life and chose rather to listen to his wife Jezebel a rebellious woman. By so doing, he alienated himself from God. He lost his kingdom, and also His life in the end. You have to know God individually.

PERSONAL CALL

God calls each of us individually to minister in our

own unique way. You may be married but God can still call you as an individual, as much as you are to work together to complement one another. You are to support each other's vision. Husbands I encourage you to release you to release your wives to serve God, because before you met her, God had called her. She belonged to Him, long before she belonged to you. And for single sisters, this call will release you from needing to search for a marriage partner in order to gain falsely assumed credibility. This will also release wives from being dependant on their husband's callings. Don't just sit there and wait for your husband's destiny to be fulfilled, woman! You have so much in you, so why do you have to wait for your husband to answer God's call? Respond to God's personal call for your life.

Get to know God individually; answer His call. Have you given your life to God? If not you had better do so. You can never succeed in life without inviting Christ in your heart. Why not invite Christ in your heart today? Put down the book and invite Christ now by praying this prayer below:

Lord Jesus I am sorry for the things I have done wrong in my life. I ask for your forgiveness and now turn from everything that I know is wrong. Thank you for dying on the cross for me to set me free from my sins. Please come into my life and fill me with your Holy Spirit and be with me forever. I commit my marriage into your hands, come and be in the centre of my marriage. Amen. Thank you.

Chapter 7

CARRY YOUR CROSS

There's a cross to carry in your marriage. If you are going to follow Christ, you must carry your cross. The cross here is a metaphor for marriage, by this I mean that marriage is a sacrifice you make to succeed. There will be opposition in your marriage, but carry your cross, stay in your marriage; God has provided sufficient grace for you, as a child of God. After the honeymoon is over, issues will begin to crop up including, first baby, bills, in-laws, division of labor and so on. A lot of challenges will begin to demand the attention of both you and your spouse. You may start to wonder whether you made the right decision to get married. This is the time you have to stand; it's time to carry your cross. Remember the words of the Lord:

"And whosoever doth not bear his cross, and come after me, cannot be my disciple. For which of you, intending to build a tower, sitteth not down first, and counteth the cost, whether he have sufficient to finish it? Lest haply, after he hath laid the foundation, and is not able to finish it, all that behold it begin to mock him, Saying, This man began to build, and was not

able to finish. Or what king, going to make war against another king, sitteth not down first, and consulteth whether he be able with ten thousand to meet him that cometh against him with twenty thousand?" Luke 14:27-31

Carrying your cross will involve the following:

Knowing God Intimately

If you want to experience a happy marriage, you both need to know your God intimately and individually. King David said in Psalms 27:4:

"One thing have I desired of the LORD, that will I seek after; that I may dwell in the house of the LORD all the days of my life, to behold the beauty of the LORD, and to enquire in his temple"

You have to seek God continually, desiring to be in His presence always; not some times, and not when you feel like it, but all the time. As the psalmist said, we need to *dwell* in the presence of the Most High God (Psalm 91:1). Not to visit; you cannot just jump in and out of the Lord's presence. You are to stay there, meditate and create a relationship with Him. The word "dwell" comes from a Hebrew word *"yaw-shab"*. It means to sit down quietly, to remain; causatively to settle, to marry the presence of God. When you marry someone, you spend time with them, kiss, hug, romance. That's exactly what you do when you marry the presence of God; sing for Him, forget about the bills and worries, and worship Him. Allow Him to be your focus without any distractions.

You need to get from the level of a baby Christian, just going to church on Sunday. Seek Him daily. This means you need to crave, pursue and go after God with all of your might, with all your heart. If we allow anything to come between us and God, we may lose it. Whether it be a job, money or spouse, you lose everything. Put God first in everything. Matthew 6:3 KJV. God can allow you to be lonely so that He can be closer to you. The Holy Spirit stays in close communication with us, He never forsakes us. God enjoys our fellowship. At times when you see things not working out, it's definitely because you are not in enough fellowship with God.

There are many couples that are not happy in their marriages because they don't acknowledge God, neither do they pursue His presence on a daily basis. As you seek God daily, you will be filled with His love, forgiveness, peace … and the list goes on and on. Your love will overflow and you will be able to show love to your spouse and others. You will even be able to forgive your spouses when they do wrong. Always be in God's presence and 'tithe' your words. What are your first words in the morning? Do you use words like

"Oh no, I am still in this marriage, why did I marry you?" What is the first thing you say when under pressure? When you receive an unfavourable medical diagnosis, what do you say? "Here we go again." Use your words to confess God's word over your marriage, and in relation to your spouse's life. The Bible gives you what to say. Go for it.

God's Word

Reading God's word gives you life and brings life in your marriage. God's word is spirit and life (John 6:63). For you to be contented in your marriage you need to read God's word; daily then you will also enjoy a vital relationship with God. God's word will put you in line, guide you and help you in your marriage with how to handle each other in different situations. Read the book of Proverbs everyday. It has 31 chapters, you can read a chapter a day, and complete the entire book in a month. Proverbs is useful in helping to deal with issues concerning our character, and it addresses matters you deal with in everyday life. Some of us wake up and go to the computer to check emails or to start chatting instead of reading God's word and praying. When you fellowship with God your spirit will be sensitive and in tune with the Holy Spirit.

When you spend time in God's word, you develop a relationship with Him. You will grow spiritually and your marriage will be positively impacted. As you consistently read, you will get to a point where you understand more of the word and will be able to apply it more effectively in your marriage. You will have great fellowship with Him, He will talk to you and you, in return, will live more harmoniously with your spouse. Not every body is willing to study God's word or even pray daily. People want an easy life; many are not willing to pay the price that brings them near to God. The Bible says, "Draw near to God and He will draw near to you…" James 4:8. The more you draw near to Him, the more you become like Him and the more your relationship and marriage will blossom (Romans 5:5). Failure to develop a good relationship with God will cause your marriage to suffer, your lives will be miserable and things will not work out as they should.

Serve God

If you want peace in your relationship, serve God. Serving God is part of carrying the cross. Jesus came to be a servant and to give his life as a ransom for many. Do you remember when He washed the feet of His disciples? *After that He poureth water into a basin, and began to wash the disciples' feet, and to wipe them with the towel wherewith he was girded. John 13:5 −14.* Serving others shows humility and selflessness. True greatness is measured in terms of service.

"But seek all of you first the kingdom of God, and His righteousness; and all these things shall be added unto you." Mathew 6:33

If you want to enjoy your life and marriage, seek God's kingdom first. As a Christian, your first priority is to seek, find, and follow the will of God. Let God have the first place and let Him be in charge of your lives.

Do the will of God, and answer His call. As a married couple do not hinder each other in serving God. Do not become a stumbling block before God. I have seen husbands or wives who hinder their partners in serving God. When you do so, you put your relationship and your own life in danger. Support each other's vision but never overdo it - be balanced! In my other book, "Woman you are great". In it, I discuss the topic of a balanced woman in great detail.

You have to have the right attitude with God; this means you should have the desire to please God no matter what. Do not allow anything to come between you, or your spouse that will hinder God's presence in your life. When you seek God's Kingdom, then everything will follow, and that includes peace in your marriage. God will give you more love than ever before; your business will prosper; if you lead a church, it too will grow and prosper spiritually.

Everything in your life will work out.

Even for those of you that are single, serve God. When Abraham's assistant was sent to find a bride for Isaac, he asked God for a sign to confirm his choice. He said that the woman who would voluntarily offer him and his camels a drink of water would be the one. Do you have any idea how much water one thirsty camel can drink? Abraham's assistant was looking for someone who wanted to serve rather than be served. In a 'me first' world that is hard to find! Notice Rebecca's qualifications. She was motivated and time conscious: 'She…ran to the well.' She was thorough: 'She drew water for all his camels' (Genesis 24:20). That one act of kindness altered the rest of her life. She had been to that well many times before and nothing unusual happened. But that day, she found favor and her life changed for good. What if she had missed her opportunity, or said, 'That's not my responsibility?' Whether you realise it or not, your actions and attitudes are determining your future. So perform with excellence because someone is watching; live by the Rebecca principle; always do more than is required of you and do it gladly!

Pray Together

Most couples pray together, only at meal times. This is not enough! That is why many of our marriages end up in divorce. The Christian divorce rate is like that of non-believers. If you want your marriage to last, share your Christian experience. Pray together, read the Bible together and go to church together. Like Joshua said, *"As for me and my house, we will serve the Lord." Joshua 24:15.*

'Pray without ceasing.' 1 Thessalonians 5:17, God listens when we pray and we He works! You can pray for anything, and if you believe you receive, you will have it. (Mark 11:24). As long as you pray with a right motive, (without selfishness) the Lord, with no doubt, will answer you. Selfish prayers are prayers where your motive to pray for you partner is for your own gain, not because you want your spouse to change and glorify God. You want them to be what you want, not what God what's them to be. "Okay Pastor J, How should I pray then?" Pray in the Spirit (in tongues) and pray God's will into your partner's life, using the word of God. God knows what needs to be changed in your partner's life, in your children's lives and so on. He is all knowing so He has no answers for you? I assure you they are there, you just need to reach out and speak to Him and hear His voice.

Pray for other couples; by sowing this seed you will reap the prayers of others concerning your own marriage. Whilst you are praying for others, do not become judgmental or speculate what their problems may be. It is so easy to be judgmental and come up with your own conclusion that 'the wife is in the wrong or vice versa.' You do not live with them, how do you know who is right? In some cases you can know who is wrong, but there are issues where you cannot tell who is in the wrong. That is why it's important to pray for them in the spirit and using God's word.

"I sought for a man among them who would...stand in the gap before Me on behalf of the land, that I should not destroy it; but I found no one." Ezekiel 22:30

Stand in the gap for others. Consider the verse above, God looked for a man who would stand in the gap for the land but there was none. Can it be the same story in our day today, that God is looking for a man who can stand in the gap to pray for marriages, nations but there is none? It is definitely possible! That's why we need to wake up and pray without ceasing.

Upon learning that Sodom and Gomorrah were going to be destroyed, Abraham did not rush to warn the cities. No, he chose to '... (Remain) standing before the Lord' (Genesis 18:22). When God said the golden calf warranted a nationwide death penalty for Israel, Moses interceded and saved the people. One translation of Exodus 32:11 says, 'Moses soothed the face of his God.' An obscure priest by the name of

Phinehas begged God not to send the plague, to destroy the people, and his prayer was heeded (see Psalms 106:30).

You might think "Why place such a premium on praying together?" The simple answer is, because when we pray, God works! Scripture says "When two of you get together on anything…and pray about it, God in heaven goes into action" (Matthew 18:19). Does any other activity promise such results? Did God call us to preach without ceasing? Or have revival meetings without ceasing? No. But He did call us to 'pray without ceasing.'

You should pray for unity in your home. It is God who will give you unity and peace in your home. The hand of God was on Judah to give them singleness of heart, to obey the command of the king and the leaders, at the word of the Lord (2 Chronicles 30:12). He gave the people a heart of unity to obey His commands. God's hand rested on the people of Judah and they walked in harmony with each other. May God's hand rest on you, your spouse and all your children, that you will all walk in unity! When you walk in unity, you accomplish much. In decision making you need to walk in unity and if you disagree on an issue, take it to God in prayer. When football legend David Beckham and his wife Victoria chose to leave Spain and head to California, some people misunderstood his decision.

But I personally thought what he did was right because in his speech, he mentioned that he was influenced by his family. It means he loves and respects his family. He knows the power of team spirit; he knows that his family is first place in his life. Your family is very important. David Beckham said the decision to quit Spain had been extremely difficult, adding that he had relied heavily on the advice of his wife and family.

Chapter 8

FRUIT OF THE HOLY SPIRIT

Without the Holy Spirit helping me in my own marriage, I can hardly imagine what condition it would be in today! But thanks to Jesus who left us the Holy Spirit to guide, instruct and comfort us, we are still standing. The word comfort comes from the Greek word "parakletos," which means, "the one alongside to help." The Holy Spirit empowers and strengthens me everyday to walk a holy life. When we need to make important decisions as a couple, we pray together to receive counsel from the Holy Spirit.

"And I will pray the Father, and He will give you another Helper, that He may abide with you forever..." John 14:16

The Holy Spirit works in order, I always ask Him to bring order in my life and marriage. It is so hard to be a wife, mother, pastor, author and itinerary minister. What a challenge! How can one balance these roles apart from relying on the Holy Spirit? Without Him helping me today, I would be living in total anarchy. He has taught me to strike a balance by exercising His fruits:

love, joy, peace, kindness and so on. Galatians 5:22.
The earth was without form, it was empty. But as the
Holy Spirit moved, hovering and brooding over it, He
brought order out of chaos (Genesis 1:2). Why not
allow the Holy Spirit to bring order in your own home?

As a Christian, you are expected to exercise the fruit of
the Holy Spirit in your marriage. Marriage is the sand
paper of the Holy Spirit. 'Give honor to marriage and
remain faithful...' (Hebrews 13:4). In this chapter we
will focus on love because love is the foundation of
marriage. "And now abide faith, hope, love, these three;
but the greatest of these is love" (1 Corinthians 13:13).
Love has everything. You cannot be kind unless you
have love; you cannot be long suffering without love. All
in all, love is the ultimate power.

*"If you abide in Me, and My words abide in you, you
will ask what you desire, and it shall be done for you.
By this My Father is glorified, that you bear much fruit;
so you will be My disciples." John 15:7*

God is glorified when you bear and exercise the fruit of
His Spirit. Jesus said you would be His disciples and a
good disciple of Christ has to display the fruit of the
Holy Spirit. Let's look at the word 'Abide'. It comes
from a Greek word that means to stay, (in a given
place), continue, dwell, endure, be present, remain,
stand, and tarry.

Jesus meant that if you abide, (meaning if you stay in Him and His words dwell in you) whatever you desire will be given to you. To abide also means to tarry. When you tarry in His presence, you will bear much fruit inside you. For you to walk in the fruit of the Holy Spirit, you need to remain in Christ, continuously walking with Him. He will strengthen you to endure all hardships, you don't give up, you exercise the fruit of patience, self control and then whatever you ask God, He will give it to you. Abide means to endure. God expects you to endure what you go through in this life, in your marriage. Abide also means to stay. Stay in Christ then you will be able to stay in your marriage even in the times of storms or tornados because you are on a strong foundation; Christ. His Spirit will help you exercise the fruit of love, patience and kindness. In the end you will be able to stand.

"You did not choose Me, but I chose you and appointed you that you should go and bear fruit, and that your fruit should remain, that whatever you ask the Father in My name He may give you." John 15:16 NKJV

God has chosen both of you to bear fruit. Bear comes from a Greek word "phero". It means to bring forth, the fruit of the Holy Spirit. Since you are born of the Spirit, let your partner see your kindness, your love. Abide also means to 'be driven,' you should be driven by the fruit of love in whatever you do for each other as a couple; and as you do that, the fruit will remain in you, and whatever you ask in His Father's name, Jesus promised, His Father would give it to you.

"But the fruit of the Spirit is love, joy, peace, longsuffering, kindness, goodness, faithfulness, gentleness, self-control. Against such there is no law."
Galatians 5:22

It is the Holy Spirit that brings forth divine character in you and your partner, all you have to do is let Him in. We have the best teacher. One of the symbols of the Holy Spirit is oil and we all know that oil heals. When you allow him to work in your marriage and your lives, you will receive an oil of easiness, by this I mean an overwhelming sense of fulfillment and ease. Things will fall in place. His anointing oil will heal your wounds and your marriage. You will not have to strive or even compete with each other, you will start to see changes in both of you that will help you live together in harmony.

LOVE

If you want to have a strong marriage relationship, you need to have unreserved love, genuine love, heartfelt love, love that stands with someone through thick and thin, 'till-death-us do-part.' Love will give you an intense desire to please God and to do good to mankind. Love is the very soul and spirit of all true Christianity; the fulfilling of the law, and what gives energy to faith itself. We are commanded in scriptures to love one another as Jesus loves us.

"This is My commandment, that you love one another as I have loved you. Greater love has no one than this, than to lay down one's life for his friends." John 15:12

Husband and wives are to love each other with the kind of unreserved love that leads them to honor each other, to esteem each other, to consider each other's welfare above their own, and to stay by each other's side through the highs and lows and the ups and downs that come in every married life. Husbands are specifically told to love their wives.

"Husbands, love your wives, just as Christ also loved the church and gave Himself for her..." Ephesians 5:25

Wives are not exempted from loving their husbands either. The older women of Crete were told to teach the younger women to love their husbands (Titus 2:4). One thing I have realised in our marriage is, my love for my husband grows everyday, and vice versa; it doesn't happen automatically, but we work towards it.

Let us look at the Christian love in 1 Corinthians 13. Although the love defined in these familiar verses are true of all relationships, it may be especially applied to a marital relationship:

• *Love is patient;* be patient with your spouse, love your spouse the way they are.

• *Love is kind;* husbands help your wife with domestic duties, share your conjical roles.

• *Love does not envy;* but celebrates - even if she has a better job than yours, men.

• *Love does not boast about being the bread winner,* or being more educated than your partner.

• *Love is not proud;* when in the wrong, admit it.

• *Love is not rude;* even when you fall out, you should keep you diague polite and respectful.

• *Love is not self-seeking;* when you go out shopping, consider your partner.

• *Love is not easily angered;* and doesn't even raise its voice or lose it's temper.

• *Love keeps no record of wrongs;* forgive and move on. Throw away that dairy with the records of all the wrong doing from the past.

• *Love does not delight in evil;* be willing to speak the truth, and comfort your spouse with the truth.

• *Love rejoices with the truth;* however much it hurts, rejoice when your partner confronts you, it's for your good.

• *Love always protects;* don't expose your partner but you pray for them.

• *Love always trusts;* don't be unduly suspicious of your partner, rather believe them knowing, you have built trust between.

• *Love always hopes;* even when things are not adding up to what you expected, continue to hope for the best.

• *Love always perseveres;* wait patiently on your unbelieving spouse.

• *Love never fails;* even when your partner is seriously ill or becomes broke, or challenged in other ways - stand by them.

By now you may be saying, Pastor Josephine, "I've done everything but my partner doesn't appreciate me? How can I keep on loving when my spouse doesn't love me in return?" Are you a disheartened partner in a relationship? Keep on loving through all circumstances you may not see any change in your partner, but it will give your spouse every reason to realise that you are still there for from them.

"Relationships are one of our greatest assets, and God wants us to value them," says Joyce Meyer. Treat your marriage carefully, be cautious when handling it. Love is an effort, put effort in to your love towards your partner. One of the ways we honor God is when we honor our partners. Correct your partner in love; deliver it with a loving tone of voice and facial expression.

These principles of love aren't given just to make marriage work. They are given to us by a wise heavenly Father who, above all, wants us to be in a good relationship with Him.

Yes, it's hard to love when all the love seems to be flowing one way. It is hard when you are the only one doing the giving, the sacrificing, the holding on. It is hard when your partner's ego or pride or selfishness means your love is not returned. You've tried talking about it but nothing happens. Ask God for more grace; grace is supplieed for you to keep on going.

If you're challenged in this area, it might help you to think about the Lord Jesus suffering for us. If anyone ever had a reason to stop loving, He did. But He loved us without reservation, even to the point of dying on the cross on our behalf. That is the kind of love we are to have for one another. It can be so hard to love someone who never understands the love of God, especially an unbelieving partner. How can you love them? Let us look at this matter in next chapter.

Chapter 9

TRANSFORMING GRACE

"Be anxious for nothing, but in everything by prayer and supplication, with thanksgiving, let your requests be made known to God; and the peace of God, which surpasses all understanding, will guard your hearts and minds through Christ Jesus." *Philippians 4:6*

UNBELIEVING SPOUSES

Do you have an unbelieving spouse? If so, do not give up on praying for their salvation. It may be years before you see a turnaround, but trust God - He is faithful. He will save them. When you pray, things are birthed in the spiritual realm. You should neither preach at them nor play Holy Spirit. Remember, it is not your job to convict your partner; that is the Holy Spirit's role. You could however, do what I did when I was in a similar situation: I prayed for my husband everyday. I would wait and when he fell asleep, lay my hands on him; praying against principalities and powers that were hindering him from getting saved. by prayer I took captive his mind, to the obedience of Christ. At the same time, I asked God to work on my conduct. I also yielded to the Holy Spirit. But of course I had tried judging, condemning and criticising him before. None of those methods worked.

I tried all I could; only to hear God say, "I am the potter." I suggest therefore that you stay in peace. Don't try to control your partner, no matter how hard you try, you can never change any one - only God can.

"For by grace you have been saved through faith, and that not of yourselves; it is the gift of God, not of works, lest anyone should boast." Ephesians 2:8-9

The Holy Spirit ministered to me through the scripture above, telling me "it was God's grace that opened my eyes to receive Christ. And though my sins were blotted out it was not down to me, therefore I could not attribute this to myself. I had no right to judge my husband." This settled everything for me. I was shocked, I cried in God's presence and repented. My breakthrough started unfolding that day after my heart had been ministered to. I saw God's transforming grace start to work in Peter's life. God will change your partner if you can stay in His presence, stay focused and believe. Moses stayed in God's presence and was transformed. Understand that it is only by God's grace that we are saved. See your spouse with the eye of grace. And if they are not yet a child of God, remember that you were not always seved, but by God's grace you were transformed. Be merciful to your mate. For he who is merciful shall obtained mercy. And as we are not perfect ourselves, there will come a time when we too need our spouses to show mercy to us. Believe that God will remove their stony heart, and give them a heart of flesh in time. If God can change the heart of a king, how much more will He change our spouse? Nothing is impossible with God! Lay your hands on your unsaved spouse and pray prayers of encouragement. When praying for your spouse to be shared, be mindful of your own conduct. Your life should be exemplary.

The Holy Spirit also led me to read Daniel 10:10-13. My eyes were again opened to understand my battle was spiritual. God had answered Daniel's prayer and sent him an angel, but the messenger angel encountered the ruling satanic prince of Persia. This spirit hindered the angel from delivering Daniel's answer to his prayer. But thank God; Daniel did not give up. Do not give up on your partner. Rather, continue to lift your spouse to the throne room of God.

Be discrete when you cast out demons from your partne's life, avoid do this in their hearing. Get tough in the spirit, like Daniel. Be consistent in prayer.

Be wise to the devil's devices. As you pray God will enlighten you to the devils plans, and will expose the strategy of the evil one. *"For what man knows the things of a man except the spirit of the man which is in him? Even so, no one knows the things of God except the Spirit of God"* (1 Corinthians 2:11).

As I tarried in prayer one day, I felt that the demon that was holding my husband had been destroyed. God saved my husband. Today he is serving the Lord, tongue speaking, demon-chasing and heaven bound. So shall it be with your partner.

Marriage is about caring for each other, whether your spouse is a believer or not. It is about wanting to please your spouse (1 Corinthians 7:34). Marriage is about giving, not taking. Give love to your partner and your love will win their heart. If you ask God, He'll give you the grace to minister to your spouse. Be patient! It's a process. If you ask God, He will give you the oil of compassion and the wine of love to pour into their wounds; and will thereby increase your influence over them. This will help you win them for God.

Our conduct will change our spouses. How you treat your wife will determine whether she follows your God. And how you treat your husband will determine how much he will want to know God. Let's look at some of the things that hinder our partners from coming to the Lord, in more detail:

1. CONDUCT

"Likewise, ye wives, be in subjection to your own husbands; that, if any obey not the word, they also may without the word be won by the conversation of the wives; while they behold your chaste conversation coupled with fear." 1 Peter 3:1

The word "Conversation" from the Greek word means manner of life, conduct, behavior, deportment.

Peter instructed us in voluntary submission to our husbands. For wives married to nonbelievers, your devout Christian behavior will influence your husbands to become Christians themselves. Husbands are to demonstrate their self-giving love for their wives whether they are Christians or not by honoring them and showing them respect.

Some theologians have expressed surprise at the fact that Peter would devote six verses to the wife, while instructing the husband in only once. I believe Peter was led by the Spirit of God to write in this way because of wives who were already married before conversion, and who were married to their husbands who were still unbelievers. They were eager for their husbands to be converted, and therefore was the danger of being impatient and becoming an authoritative preacher at home instead of being a submissive, winsome wife as God intended. And yet the one-verse message to the husband is deep and full, containing much of what he needs to make his home a little paradise on earth.

- CRITICISM

One of the ways that my conduct was hindering Peter was down to my being so critical and nagging towards him. I wanted him to pray and read the Bible like I did; not knowing I was irritating him. Your partner might not know how to pray but you can pray on his behalf, until he became better at it. When my husband came to the Lord, I was very excited. When we got down to pray, being an intercessor, I thought I was going to pray for long hours with him, not knowing that he was spiritually young. He could only pray for a few minutes. Instead of appreciating him, I started attacking him. I almost lost my breakthrough, until the Holy Spirit warned me to just leave him, and I let the Holy Spirit teach him how to pray. Gradually this worked; in God's timing, my husband learnt how to pray. Avoid being critical of your partner. Appreciate the little he or she does. And trust God to change them for the better, little by little.

Remember that you are a friend, not a mentor. Don't try to change your spouse by nagging; or asking, 'Why can't you pray like me?' Or, 'why do you always refuse to come to church?' This is more like parenting than partnering. Tell them once what's bothering you, not a-thousand times! Ask yourself, "Would I say this to a valued friend?" If not, don't say it.

Some women act as though when they got saved they were exempted from submitting to their husbands, and I once subscribed to that myself. Due to the eternal importance of salvation, I thought my main responsibility at home was to aggressively preach to Peter in order to drive him to Christ. I became a fiery preacher, lecturing him on ways he must never offend Christ. On the contrary, a wife's duty is to submit to the husband and to serve in love. *"Likewise, ye wives, be in subjection to your own husbands" 1 Peter 3:1*

If it is the wife who is not saved, the husband too has to endeavor to win her to Christ without aggressive preaching, but with faithfulness, love, care, honor and respect. The power of consistent righteousness can eventually draw the wife or husband to Christ. Make a spouse develop interest in the word of God and desire to have salvation, and a life transformation. A pure life has great power and influence to make others want to listen to the gospel and get saved.

Don't force your spouse to go to church. Allow God to work ion them, in His way. It is not by might nor by power, but by the Holy Spirit. The two of you can pray prayers of agreement. God will still hear your prayers; He understands that your partner is still spiritually young. This is what God told me to do with my husband - pray a prayer of agreement with him everyday. It is also a prayer of unity because you are praying together and you are in agreement. A prayer of agreement is not necessarily a long prayer that should last an hour - no! Even a five minute prayer with someone spiritually young is honoured by God. It is also a prayer of power. Appreciate the little your partner does. Even your spouse refuses to pray with you, don't fight over it. Rather, pray for them, even in their hearing. As I did this, I saw my husband change by the grace of God. Today he is a God-fearing man who loves Jesus with a passion. Well, you might say Jesus prayed for long hours. It is true. There is a day Jesus prayed until the fourth watch. "A watch" constitutes three hours. But there were also times when He prayed for a few minutes. When Jesus prayed to His Father about raising Lazarus in John 11:41–42, it was a short prayer yet God heard His prayer. Your main aim is to be led by God. He will give you wisdom to pray for as long or as little as you need to.

2. OVER SPIRITUALITY

Before your spouse became a man or woman of God, they were first and foremost, human beings, with real physical and mental needs. Husband, your wife needs you. We are still living on earth. You might say sister

J, "We are not of the world. We were raised with Christ; we are to seek those things which are above, where Christ is sitting at the right hand of God, according to 1 Colossians 3:1-2." Yes, I believe you a hundred percent but remember, you still live in this world. You therefore must use wisdom in whatever you do. The same scriptures say, *"Dishonest scales are an abomination to the Lord, but a just weight is His delight." Proverbs 11:1*

On one occasion I woke up to pray at around 4:00 am and as I began, the Holy Spirit told me to shut up. At one point I thought it was the devil trying to distract me. But the voice continued, until I kept quiet. He said to me "I hate dishonest scales." 'What do you mean Lord?' I asked. "Were you in agreement with your husband when you came to talk to me? Did you do your duty as a wife? When do you clean your house? When do you spend time with your kids? Why do you always have to be involved in every department in church? Did I call you to be everywhere? Be a balanced woman."

When the Holy Spirit opened my eyes to see that I was unbalanced, I was shocked. I had been serving the Lord with all my heart but lacked wisdom and knowledge. I was so busy serving God that I had neglected my family. I was in the choir, counseling department, intercession, evangelism, to mention but a few. When it came to my family, I was rarely there. But the Bible makes us to understand in *Proverbs 20:23 "Diverse weights are an abomination to the Lord, and dishonest scales are not good."* It glorifies God when we live a balanced lifestyle.

God hates dishonest or unjust scales. He is a God of order. An honest scale is a symbol of justice, representing equality and fairness. A balanced scale is considered to be just. But an unbalanced scale indicates that it has been tipped unfairly in one direction. Its reading then becomes unreliable.

When your wife comes back from the saloon and finds you watching a Christian program, please stop or pause it and compliment her. This will make her feel loved and appreciated. See how Christ treats the church and treats you. God has blessed you, and He compliments you in His word saying, you are a chosen generation, a royal priesthood, a holy nation, His own special people (1 Peter 2:9).

Have some fun; even your children will be bored by your spirituality if you over do it. The Bible teaches that we're not to be so spiritual that we become unavailable. God says, 'I want those who are married to be concerned about pleasing their spouse.' Your first ministry is to your own home... your first calling is to your own spouse. Your priorities need to start there;

then they can spread to your career, your vocation and other pursuits.

Change the atmosphere in your home. Don't get carried away in too much spirituality. Some wives spend the whole month fasting, even when their husband needs them, they are busy with spiritual authority. A non-believing husband can grow to resent your God because he doesn't understand the things of the Spirit, and may feel that you neglect his needs. Even a believing husband does not deserve to be starved of time and attention. Always agree on what you do.

Some people become so spiritual that when you pay them a compliment like "you're so attractive," they think you're being carnal. I once had someone make a comment about a lady pastor who was teaching on the physical beauty and health of a woman. She said, "The pastor has a narrow brain, why is she only speaking about physical beauty, and watching our weights?" Why are we judgmental? What wrong did the woman of God say? Why are we not willing to learn from others? The pastor was asked to speak on physical beauty and health; losing weight and the like. But this lady, in her ignorance quickly jumped to the conclusion that the woman of God was narrow minded. Hey sis! We have spent a lot of time preaching about what goes on on the inside; so dedicating time to health and beauty is not carnal. We need to strike a balance. We can become so spiritual that we make looking attractive a sin. Living a balanced lifestyle will bring out the best in your marriage. And when your marriage is going well, God gets the glory.

3. FAILING TO UNDERSTAND THE DIFFERENT SPIRITUAL LEVELS

John writes, "Do not love the world..." even though the Bible commands us not to love the world, it doesn't mean that we are to be so heavenly minded that we are of no earthly value. Loving the Lord more doesn't mean loving your partner or family around you less; or feeling awkward around them; or losing touch with them; or not knowing how to communicate with them; or alienating them by giving off signals that you are somehow spiritually superior to them.

Both of you may not be at the same spiritual level. Your spouse may be a recent convert. Don't force him/her to pray with you; take one day at a time. You will notice that your prayer levels are different. When praying, don't start casting demons out of him. A friend of mine tells me, one day she was praying while her husband who was not a believer was in bed but awake. She prayed for him, saying, "Father l thank you for my husband, bless him. l come against the demons in him". Before she could even finish praying, the man sat up and said to her, "Since when did l turn into a demon? Who do you think you are? Is that what they teach you in church? If l ever hear you call me a demon again, that will be the end. l have heard enough of you, always waking up in the morning and shouting in prayers, at night the same story. Can't you ever pray silently or control you voice?" The man was right, first you can't cast demons out of your partner who is not a believer, just like that. First, they don't understand the things of the Spirit. Even if they did, it would be wise to pray in your heart or even in tongues. You can cast out demons in the Spirit. Besides, why shout when praying? Won't God hear you when you pray silently? He understands and sees your heart.

Please don't only talk about the Bible and spiritual stuff, rather, be balanced or else you will make your mate feel bored. Talk about day-to-day life, your love, children, sports, etc. God will not be upset. Don't be so heavenly minded that you're of no earthly value. Loving the Lord more doesn't mean loving your partner less, or feeling awkward around them, or losing touch with them, or alienating them by giving signals that you are somehow spiritually superior to them.

When your partner eventually comes to God, strike a balance in everything you do. You would also benefit if you planned to attend our women's conference; "The balanced woman class," during which l teach women to be balanced in all the areas of life. At church, be wise and don't cuddle members of the opposite sex. Your partner may read it differently. That could precipitate a war when you get back home.

4. BEING IMPATIENT

"Let patience have her perfect work, that ye may be [mature]...wanting nothing." James 1:4

Just because it hasn't happened yet, doesn't mean God has changed His mind to save your man. While you are waiting - God is working. Impatience is a sign of immaturity. It is children who don't have patience for anything! So, are you being childish or showing maturity? God sets His watch to accomplish His purpose, not ours. Paul writes: 'We know that all things work...according to His purpose' (Romans 8:28). When you understand God's purpose, you won't permit things that are contrary to it, including hurry and worry you will allow God to do His work according to his timing. And what are we supposed to do while we are waiting? Listen to me, 'Though the fig tree does not bud and there are no grapes on the vines, though the olive crop fails and the fields produce no food, though there are no sheep in the pen and no cattle in the stalls, yet I will rejoice in the Lord, I will be joyful in God my Savior' (Habakkuk 3:17-18). Begin thanking God today for what He's done in your partner's life so far, and what He's going to do in their life, because He will - He absolutely will, come through for you!

5. FAILURE TO CONFESS GOD'S WORD IN YOUR PARTNER'S LIFE

Continue confessing positive things in your spouses' life, by faith. Confess victory even before you see transformation. Hold fast to your confession of faith without wavering. Circumstances might get worse after confessing but continue, don't give up. Gideon and his three hundred fighters shouted victory they won their battle and as a result the enemy became frightened; and the Midianities killed each other (Judges 7:18-22).

"And they overcame him by the blood of the Lamb, and by the word of their testimony; and they loved not their lives unto the death." Revelation 12:11

The word Confess is a Greek word meaning "to agree with or to speak the same language." If you confess what God's word says about your life, or the life of your child or spouse, your confession will bear fruit. God's word is powerful!

So many times I hear couples say when asked, how is your partner? "He is getting worse, am fed up, I have prayed and nothing is happening," or "She is not interested in this church stuff, I am not bothered any more." Watch what you say! You are not called to walk by what you see but by faith. By faith everyday, I made positive confession over Peter's life. If someone came and asked me, "How is your husband? I would say, "He is a mighty man of God. God is doing great things in his life." I wasn't lying, I saw him in the spirit, not in the physical, and finally what I saw in the spirit came to pass in the natural. Today he is a mighty man of God, he is a teacher of God's word. Hallelujah!

What you do with your mouth is very important. Your mouth was not given to you for eating only; it is also your instrument for charting the course of your life. The Lord Jesus showed us the immense power that can be released when we use our tongues the right way. On a certain occasion, Jesus went to a fig tree, hoping to get some fruit to eat. The Bible says, *"When He came to it, He found nothing but leaves; for the time of fig was not yet. And Jesus answered and said unto it, No man eat fruit of thee hereafter for ever….."* Mark 11: 13-14.

Isn't it very striking that the Bible says, Jesus answered' and not 'Jesus said'. There is no record of who talked to Jesus, so what did He respond to? You see, everything God made has intelligence; if you are therefore faced with a situation which is unfavorable, you have to respond to that situation with words.

When He awoke on a boat to a stormy sea, He spoke to the wind and the waves (Mark 7: 39), and they heard Him, when He was confronted with deaf ears, He spoke to the deaf ears (Mark 7:34); the ears weren't deaf to the word of God. He spoke to fish; He spoke to bread, and even to a corpse. ... I could go on and on.

Everyday, you must have regular 'talking sessions' whereby you stay alone and declare the word of God over your life and over every situation that you face. Talk to your body, to your unbelieving partner, to your bank account, talk into your children's lives, and talk to your home. Speak God's word over them! Declare that you are what God says you are; that your spouse is what God says they are. Practice these 'talking sessions' everyday and watch your marriage and your life, go from glory to glory. The situation may seem as if it's not changing, but it has heard you and it will conform to the word of God, eventually.

Right now, put what I have just said into practice by praying this prayer:

Dear Father, thank you for putting the power to

change things in my mouth! I decree and declare that I am making progress and moving forward and upward in the name of Jesus. My partner is saved; I am full of divine health, full of prosperity and full of joy! Thank you Lord! Amen.

6. LACK OF WISDOM

"If any of you lacks wisdom, let him ask of God, who gives to all liberally and without reproach, and it will be given to him." James 1:5

Handling your spouse will take wisdom. Wisdom comes from God. Ask God for wisdom to run your home - it is His pleasure to give it you. When God revealed this to me I went ahead and asked for it. when I did He told me to cut down on some things I was doing in church and only concentrate on evangelism, preaching, and leading women. He told me to delegate other jobs I was doing. This brought tremendous results that even today my entire family is testifying the goodness of, and thanking the Lord. My children sometimes make fun out of it by saying "Mum what happened to you? These days you spend time with us, we thought you got married to the church." We laugh together everytime they remind me. Understand me, serving God is good but your involvement in church shouldn't be over done or else it can become a hindrance to your spouse and family.

Look at Jesus; He used wisdom to deal with everybody. He was able to speak to prostitutes, tax men and He made them feel special and loved. He showed them their mistakes in love and won their hearts.

Peter used to say to me, "Will you stop trying to change me; you're not going to change me, let the Holy Spirit change me if I need to change." It was hard for me to let go, I wanted to help God to change Peter, eventually one day the Holy Spirit told me to learn how to lean on Him concerning Peter and my family. He told me, what you are trying to do is the work of the Holy Spirit, you cannot change any body, it's not by might, not by power but by God's Spirit that people change. Did you know it is not always easy to change? God told me to look at my own life and see how it took years to change some habits I had, and how He was still working on me. I realised then that change isn't easy, and even right now when I look at myself, I know that I am not where I need to be, but still, I am glad I am not where I used to be. Many times I misbehaved, but thank God for the Holy Spirit, our teacher, He never gave up on me, but kept on teaching me. Then gradually, day by day I changed in one area and then another. Your partner will change in Jesus' name.

Limit your church activities and unnecessary visits to your friends from church. Some pastors hold long services and their members fail to arrive back home in time to cook for their husbands. This leads to problems in marriages and some men get fed up of the church as a result.

If your pastor holds long services, you may want to consider forming a team to present your problem to him. If there's no change, seek God on what to do, but don't lose your marriage over it. God builds the house, but we have to do our own decorating! My dear, God has released those who are married from the level of consecration He expects from those who are single, so that you will be able to spend time working on your marriage.

By now you are saying, "But I need to spend time with the Lord." True. The Bible doesn't release you from your relationship with the Lord altogether, it just sets some priorities. You are called to be committed to God - and to your partner!

Some married people decide to open up their homes to host church programs, or they bring church members who are looking for accommodation into their homes without even consulting their partners. This is not right. Whatever you do, please plan it together.

When Democratic Nancy Pelosi was voted in as the first female Speaker of the House, in her first speech she thanked her family by saying, "My family pushed me from the kitchen to the congress." She knows that her family played a big part and therefore she honored them. This is a good example for us. We should always love, honor and respect our families.

Pastors Visits

Don't visit people's homes when you haven't made an appointment. Never visit couples at awkward hours. Many wives have made a mistake of inviting their male pastors without the consent of their husbands. You could potentially put yourself into temptation. Some of these husbands are not believers and therefore they cannot understand why you do this. Even if they are believers, it is not right. Some partners give away things like land and cars without the knowledge and consent of their spouse. Some time back, a wife announced that God had instructed her to give away their land to her pastor and surrendered the title deed to him. On learning this, her husband blocked her from giving away the land. After two weeks, she had not got the land title back despite her pleas to the pastor to return it.

What the wife did was very wrong. Always consult

your spouses if God has spoken to you to give something away. If your spouse doesn't feel it, go back in prayer and ask God to speak to your partner. If God has spoken to you, He will definitely speak to your partner.

I would advise Pastor's to use wisdom when receiving gifts from a person who is married. Always ask them whether their spouses know about it. Or suggest that you are going to call them and thank them. But this also depends on what they have given you. Watch out for big gifts like cars and land.

7. OVERSERVING WEAKNESS

Even if you have an unbelieving partner, you are to respect him, love her and look beyond their weakness. Love conquerors all things. Don't look at his drinking problem, rather, see the greatness in him. Even you are not pleased with your partner's walk with the Lord, don't harass them. It's the Holy Spirit's job to judge, not yours. It's by your good behavior that will change your partner, not your preaching. I came to the Lord before my husband did. After trying everything to convince him to come to the Lord, it still didn't work. I would wake up at night and start from my previous night's 'sermon,' only to make matters worse. I placed scripture stickers all over the house; it didn't work.

What changed him finally was, loving him the way he was. No amount of nagging or pressure will help you to change your partner. Being a Christian wife or husband is not always an easy job, but it can be one of the most fulfilling.

I encourage you to love your partner Avoid name calling, have pet name for one another and pamper each other at every opportunity. *I have compared thee, O my love, to a company of horses in Pharaoh's chariots. Song of Solomon 1:9.* The woman also calls the man *"My lover."* Sarah called Abraham *"my lord"* in 1 Peter 3:6. For me, I call my husband "Dad Pet," - he loves it! Love conquerors all things.

Backslidden Spouses?

Has your partner backslidden? Don't give up. Pray for them. God desires that we have mercy towards people, especially our spouses. Jesus said, "Be ye therefore merciful, as your Father also is merciful." The reason why Jesus came is to seek and to save that which was lost, so when we fail to welcome backsliders, we have failed Jesus. We have not appreciated what He did on the cross. In fact we crucify Him again. And that's serious! We are effectively saying that the cross was not enough for these people who have backsliden.

Never forget that God loves us all, and that includes

those who backslide into sin. He loves them, but hates the sin they commit. Did your partner backslide? Please don't give up on them unless they have gone to the extreme and they are not willing to change however much you speak into their lives; for example, if they become a witch, or a homosexual, etc (Leviticus 15:10).

Chapter 10

MARRIAGE ROLES

In today's society the roles that men and women play in marriages has effectively changed, from past tradition. While driving my car one day I turned the radio on and randomly landed on a secular station. There was a discussion about roles in marriage today. The wife was being told that since she has the same rights as her husband, she doesn't have to submit to him. During the discussion, pressure was being put on husbands to take care of themselves and not to worry about their wives. It was so confusing. I felt sorry for those who were listening, who didn't know the truth; and for any husband or wife who was listening and needed direction. It became clear to me that there are married couples out there who need answers to questions concerning marital roles. Let's first look at the roles of the husband. The Bible says that the husband is the head of the wife. Paul wrote:

"But I would have you know, that the head of every man is Christ; and the head of the woman is the man; and the head of Christ is God." *1 Corinthians*

11:3

"For the husband is the head of the wife, even as Christ is the head of the church: and he is the savior of the body." Ephesians 5:23

As Christ exercises authority over the Church, so as to save and protect it, the husband is expected to exercise authority over his wife by protecting, comforting, and providing her with every necessary comfort of life, according to his power and ability.

ROLES OF A HUSBAND

Head

Marital headship does not mean that the husband is superior. The same verse that says the man is head of the woman, also says that God is the head of Christ (1 Corinthians. 11:3); yet we know they are equal in nature. Both are fully in the image of God, only the husband's headship is functional. It helps the marriage work, by cerating order. When understood and expressed in the spirit of Christ, headship fulfills the role of a servant. Headship carries with it great responsibility. The husband is to provide loving, understanding, self-sacrificing, patient, God-honoring leadership. Husbands are to have a vision for their marriage, and this vision needs to be shared with their wives. Each year the husband should update his wife on his plans for their family. For instance, plans to build or buy a new house, or to start a business venture. The family vision should be written down along with all the strategies to achieve it. Husbands and wives should come together daily to pray for the vision. Wives, do not feel inferior or try to fight for headship as some do. Your husband maybe the head of your family but you are the neck that turns his head, so you are also very important. Lean on the grace of God and respect your husband.

While this principle is one of the most misquoted and misused in scripture, it does not need to be. Biblical leadership is not dictatorial or blindly self-serving; husbands are not to be dictators, or to boss their wife around but should lead in humility. Headship is to be provided in love, before the eyes of God (Eph. 5:25; Col. 3:19). A husband, as figure head, is to lead with understanding (1 Pet. 3:7).

Some husbands are weak in the area of leading a home. Wives can help their husbands lead with wisdom. Wives should not use their influence to control their husbands. As a wife you are accountable to your husband, and should therefore keep him informed about whatever you do. Homes where wives exercise wisdom in this way are usually happy homes. The Bible says *"For the husband is the head of the wife...*" Wives can be submissive to their husbands but lead but leading with wisdom. In their decision making, they consult their husbands. To enjoy a fruitful marriage, husbands and wives should consult one another, and before making any decisions, both should come into agreement. This is true for all important issues. You might think, "what if they agree on the wrong thing?" When this happens, a couple must wait in prayer, and rely on God to intervene and bring about the best outcome.

Wives, do not demand that your husband becomes a leader in the home if they are not leading naturally. The desire for leadership has to come from inside him, as lead by the word of God and the Spirit of God. So, instead of demanding he lead, pray earnestly for him that God would awaken his true manhood, birth in him a vision, and nurture in him a desire for leadership.

A woman who does not find joy in helping a man provide loving, thoughtful leadership in the home will have problems. Even tif a woman finds it difficult to accept good initiatives from her husband, she will need to remember that her ultimate confidence and trust is in God Himself. Your marriage will have the best opportunity to succeed when both husband and wife accept their roles.

As a leader, a husband should set an example in every

area of their life. This includes paying tithes, respecting pastors and leaders in the church. If you have an issue, arrange to street or speak with them about it. If you are rebellious you will pass the same spirit to your family.

"Submit to one another out of reverence for Christ" Ephesians 5:21

We are to submit to one another out of respect and regards for God. Men, even as a leader you are also called to submit. For the husband, this submission means loving your wife so much that you give up selfishness to help your wife and strengthen her. Serve God in your own home. Jesus said if you want to be a leader then be a servant (Mathew 20:26). Jesus, the head of the church, came to serve, not to boss the church around (Mathew 20:27-28).

"And we urge you, brethren, to recognize those who labor among you, and are over you in the Lord and admonish you, to esteem them very highly in love for their work's sake. Be at peace among yourselves." 1 Thessalonians 5:12-13

We are commanded to esteem our leaders. Husbands are to set an example by esteeming the leaders in their lives. The word "esteem" comes from the Greek word 'hegeomai' it means consider. To consider means to take into account. Show regard for your pastors and leaders. If you obey your leaders in church, then your own leadership in your own home will be easy. What you sow is what you reap. Husbands set an example to your wife and children, they will follow in your footsteps.

Provide

"So husbands ought to love their own wives as their own bodies; he who loves his wife loves himself. For no one ever hated his own flesh, but nourishes and cherishes it, just as the Lord does the church." Ephesians 5:28-29

The words "nourish and cherish" are significant. The word nourish (ektrephei) from Greek is most often used in the Bible in relation to raising children and providing them with what they need. In Genesis 45:11 Joseph says to his brothers, "There I will provide (ekthreps?) for you, for there are yet five years of famine to come." So the point is that the husband who leads like Christ takes the initiative to see to it that the needs of his wife and children are met. He provides for them, as a caring and nourishing provider.

If you love your wife you will nourish and cherish her and your love for her will compel you to supply for your family, withholding no good thing from her. God gave his son Jesus Christ to the world to save it because of the unconditional love He has for the world. He sent Him to die for us, because He loved us too much to see us perish, due to a lack of a saviour.

I counseled a couple; the husband was very smartly dressed but the wife was in old clothes. It was after Sunday service. One of the wife's complaints was that her husband never provided for the family. If he tried at all, he would go to a local market and buy her second hand clothes while he always brought himself the more finer and expensive things.
This behaviour is not reflective of God's love for the church and His willingness to provide and nourish us with good things. The husband in this story was not remorseful at all. He was so arrogant in his talking, that his wife spoke with fear; she could hardly look him in the eye. She confessed that her husband used to beat her. To cut a long story short, the couple eventually separated. This man failed to meet his wife's needs by not providing her with the nourishment her soul longed for; and cherishing her as God intended. He was so stingy and narrow minded.

"A stingy man is eager to get rich and is unaware that poverty awaits him." Proverbs 28:22

How can a person be stingy to their own family? You can never be blessed in this life if you are self-centered. That is selfishness. And according to scripture, poverty awaits you. A mean and selfish person will never find contentment and peace.

Paul wrote *'...I have learned to be content...'* *Philippians 4:11*. Greed is a form of selfishness where we always focus on ourselves, and have an 'me, myself and I' mentality. It is the 'trinity' of self. Greedy people are never satisfied, and often complain and gumble. Even if there is nothing to complain about they look for it. The opposite of greed is contentment. This husband in the story above complained that he did not have enough money to better provide for his wife, while buying new clothes for himself and making his wife suffer with his kids. Even with the little that he had, he could have demonstrated his love for the family by sharing what he could.

Greed is an idol that makes you place money above God, and above your spouse and family. The Bible says, *a greedy man stirs up discord and rebellion but he who trusts in the Lord will prosper. Prov. 28:25.*

I know of a Christian lady who was very hard working. She worked as a nurse in London and was married to a greedy man. A sister she knew called her to warn her that she might be wasting time with that man. Not happy with this advice, she hung up on her. When she confronted her husband, he started beating her. As if that was not enough he also framed her and she ended up in prison. By the grace of God her parents went and got her out of prison. One thing that shocked me was, when the police asked the husband whether he wanted to take his wife home. He refused and said all he wanted from her were the keys for the house. The wife had paid for the land, built the house, she did everything and every body in the neighbourhood knew this. While she was in London, she sent money to her husband to buy the land, build the house and take care of expenses. Unfortunately the man was very greedy. After buying and building, he put all the assets in his name. So after they had settled and the wife had now decided work in their home country, the man decided to throw her out of the house. Imagine! He was after his wife's money all along. When the wife realised that this was the case, they divorced.

Demanding wives

Though God commands that husbands provide for the wives; that does not give wives license to demand things from our husbands. When a wife shows her husband that she believes in him; he is encouraged to do anything for her, and will provide her with his very best. Wives must also keep in mind that although your husband has a duty to provide; ultimately, God is your source. If God cares for the land and waters it, and enriches it abundantly, how much more will he do it for you?

"You visit the earth and water it, you greatly enrich it; the river of God is full of water; you provide their grain, for so you have prepared it." Psalms 65:9

Instread of putting demands on your husband, look up to God, He is your provider. There are many promises in the Bible that God gave us concerning provision in our lives. Your husband is not your El–Shaddai, the all sufficient one. God will always fulfill His promise to you, look up to Him, He will never give up on you, and He will never lie - no way! It might take years before you see the manifestation of God's promises in your life, but He will always honour His word and make a way for you.

What has God promised you concerning your marriage, children, business, and church? He will fulfill it, come snow or rain it shall come to pass. People may laugh and air out their evil opinions because it appears that God's promises are not working out for you, but remember that God will shut their mouths in time, so do not be overly concerned with the opinions of others.

When you believe in the promises of God, He will fulfill them in your life. He shall supply all your needs according to His riches in glory (Phillips 4:19). *For every beast of the forest is Mine, and the cattle on a thousand hills. I know all the birds of the mountains, and the wild beasts of the field are Mine. Psalms 50:10*

MARRIAGE ROLES

Some wives seldom show appreciation. When the
husband buys them a dress, they will complain that the
dress is cheap, not modern, or it is not their calibre, etc.
Women who fall into this category are not willing to
adjust; and so become hard to please. If you can
identify with this kind of behaviour, then ask you to
seriously reconsider your actions. Being in a
relationship where appreciation is not shown, can lead
to a miserable marriage. My advice to husbands is to
be transparent with your finances. If you are on a low
income, and are honest with your life, she will much
more likely be understanding if you buy her gifts that
are not too expensive. But remember that every
woman loves to be treated, so once in a while it is a
good idea to dig a little deeper in your pockets and buy
your wife something costly - she deserves it.

ROLES OF A HUSBAND

My husband's word of wisdom
I spoke to my husband about the idea of a husbands
being the provider for their family. I have included the
advice he gave in this next section of the book.

"To start with, let us build the foundation from the
word of God (Genesis 1:26-28). A man of God is the
provider (Gen. 3: 19, I Tim. 5: 8). A man is supposed
to be: a man who takes full responsibility for his
actions, is the head of his household, including his

wife, is considerate of others and obeys God's commandments. He is respectful of others, and puts God first in his life. He is a good provider and is a good father to his children. He is strong, yet restrained. He is outside the norm, because he doesn't have to do anything sinful to prove that he's macho. He does not lie, cheat, or steal, and then make excuses to justify it. He is sorry for the wrong he has done. He knows God is Spirit and needs to be worshipped. He knows the Bible, understands Christianity and that God is not to be trivialised. A good man understands commitment, fidelity, fairness, honour, responsibility, and character. That is what a man is all about.

But as the saying goes, *'it is easier said than done.'* Inevitably, it is sometimes tough to keep up with all of these expectations. For example, if a man is in a situation where he can't be the main breadwinner because his wife happens to have a better job. In such situations, it is important that both husband and wife address the situation, and make plans to change it if necessary.

Most importantly, a husband in this scenario must keep his faith strong, and at the forefront of his mind. In testing times, remain positive, keep looking for better jobs and entry points in business (if you do not have any yet); and surround yourself with those people who will bring out the best in you, rather than those who will put you down or make you feel bad about the situation.

My favourite scripture is Hebrews 11:1 - 'Now faith is the substance of things hoped for, the evidence of things not seen.' It is essential to focus on where you are going and not be confined to where you are right now, or where you have been. Do not allow your temporary troubles to define you; because where you are does not determine who you are.

"Humanity moves between the two poles: "simplicity" and "complexity." People who have the mindset that sees one clear outcome have a greater tendency towards taking vigorous action, with the things they pursue. As such they are more likely to succeed in everything they do because they do not stop to split hairs, and have abounding confidence in their own ability to get things done. On the other hand, those with sophisticated and analytical minds tend to get lost in a maze of fine distinctions. such people tend to see how complicated things really are, which reduces their conviction to take positive action to nil. Very few people manage to combine the principles of simplicity and complexity. In my view, a combination of the two is achieved with lively Christian faith, which enables this miracle to happen. Bringing together the virtue of simplicity and complexity, gives both profound understanding and simplicity of heart." (Paul Tournier 1898–1986)

Life is a journey. It is important to keep moving forward with a purpose, direction and passion, and with the fundamental aim of providing for your family.

I feel terribly bad when I fail to meet the needs of my immediate family. I thought I was alone in this but I have come to realise that many others feel the same. Often it is this very situation that tempts some to resort to lying and abandoning homes to escape responsibility, which only makes matters worse. God has not given us the spirit of fear but of power, love and a sound mind. The best thing to do when faced with the challenge of not being in the best position to provide for your family is to stay committed to your family and keep them updated with your progress; as you work to improve your circumstances.

If a man does not stand in his position of leadership – as provider, it has the potential to weaken his decision making powers.

I also ask the ladies who are privileged to have better jobs than their hubbies, thus more money to provide for the family, to pray with their husbands, build their esteem, speak to the teacher in them, and work to bring out the real man in them. God has never intended man and woman – husband and wife, to compete, but rather to complement each other. That is why God designated the woman as a helper. If a helper wants to steal the show, then there is likely to be a power struggle. This will clearly be observed by children (if any) and people close to you, it is likely to bring shame to the couple. Observers of your fighting will not respect your union.

Who is the breadwinner in your household? Are you happy the way things are? If not, are definite plans being made to bring the situation under control? These are the questions I leave with you, to think about.

Love

We have already spoken about love and I believe by now you have an understanding of what love means. God expects you to follow the example of Christ's love for the church. Love your wife as Christ loved the church. How your parents related with you will determine how you relate with your spouses. If they showed you love, it will be easy to love your spouse and if they failed to show you love, you may struggle to show love to your spouse. That's why you need to ask God to teach you how to love and to receive love.

"Husbands, love your wives, and be not bitter against them." Ephesians 5:25; Colossians 3:19.

Understanding

Study your wife, take time to know her. There are times when a woman is moody; this is the time when we are in our menstruation period. Please, do not harass her or be patient; rather, be loving towards her and allow time for her emotions to settle. And wives please, do not use this as an excuse to be moody and grumpy. Exercise self control.

"Husbands, likewise, dwell with them with understanding..." 1 Peter 3:7

If your wife is evidently unhappy, show concern. Find out why she is upset, don't just leave her and say, 'Well it's up to her; it's none of my business.' If it is not your business then whose is it? The same rules apply when she is happy. When she has a vision, support it. Sit down and listen when she shares her goals and dreams with you, she needs your support.

Honour

Honour your wife and God will honor you in due season. Do not put her down before your friends. Carry her with respect. When you are going out, open the car door for her; you have nothing to lose, when people see you they will consider you a responsible gentlemen. But of course those who are jealous of the love you share will make negative comments, like, 'The woman bewitched that man, he is so stupid, how he can stoop low to a woman like that?' And as a wife because your husband treat you with honor don't take him for granted, don't make him treat him like a Tomboy and start telling your friends, 'I have him under my feet, I can get him to do anything...' Honour your husband by respecting him, and the love he has for you.

"...giving honor to the wife, as to the weaker vessel..." 1 Peter 3:7

Give honour to your wife as unto the weaker vessel. The word honour explains that the term weaker is not a comparison of quality but an expression of sensitivity. Women are more fragile, so treat your wife with love and care. The instructions to husband to honour their wives, does not mean he loves women more than men No! Rather, God is saying your wife is more fragile; and this does not mean she is of less quality.
Marriage is a seed, it must be planted. Marriage is a plant, it must be nurtured. Marriage is a garden, it must be cultivated. Work on your relationship; don't treat your wife as a second class citizen. Wife, respect your man. That is your God-ordained duty to respect him and to help him.

GOD'S GRACE IN MARRIAGE

"And Adam gave names to all cattle, and to the fowl of the air, and to every beast of the field; but for Adam there was not found an associated helper for him."
Genesis 2: 20

God made lion, cattle and other creatures but none of them were fit enough to be Adam's companion. Some wives are like lions, they roar and bark in their homes. And their husband and children are always the prey. It is any wonder that some men stay out late at nights, in clubs and the like? On some occasions it's the attitude of their wies that put them off returning home early. It is equally important for husbands to remember to address your wife with respect, do not dish out demands to her. A good leader leads, he doesn't boss others around. Treat your wife as a queen, and not as a slave.

Husbands are also suppose to use their superior strength and experience for the benefit of their wives, and thus honor her by becoming her protector and support. Woman was formed from the rib of a man, which is postponed under his arm; this signified that a woman should enjoy his protection. When I hear any funny noise in the house at night, I immediately alert my husband who usually rises to face the challenge. I do this, not because I don't trust in God, but because of the boldness of my husband. For my protection in Peter - it is God given. I believe this principle of protection applies to all men. The word honor, signifies maintenance as well as respect: therefore a man is to maintain his wife, and provide for her.

We are known as weaker vessels, yet made strong by wisdom, grace and the fear of God. The Bible says *I can do all things through Christ who strengthens me (Philippians 4:13).* The people that know their God shall carry out great exploits, they shall not fear, they are strong in the Lord. Finally, be strong in the Lord woman of God, and trust in His mighty power. See Ephesians 6:10.

We are more delicately, and consequently, more splendidly, constructed. The wife has what the husband wants: beauty and delicacy. The husband has what the wife wants courage and strength. Each set of traits compliments the other.

Do not hold onto bitterness
Bitterness is a form of resentment. Do not resent your wife. If she annoys you so much, do not become bitter. Rather, talk to her about any issues you have with them. When you resent your wife and do not forgive her, you open yourself to demonic attack. When you do forgive, please, do not bring uphold issues again. "The only way out of the prison of resentment, is through the door of forgiveness." says Bob Gas,

author of Forgetting Your Past, and Starting Over. Bitterness will literally hinder our prayers. The apostle Peter mentioned it in 1 Peter 3:7 "...that your prayers may not be hindered."

"Husbands, love your wives and do not be bitter toward them" Colossians 3:19

Men, I speak to you on behalf of women who cannot speak out for themselves, those in whom the devil has instilled fear. Do not allow bitterness to dominate you to such a point that you start abusing your wife. Many wives are undermined, day in and day out by their husbands. They are called all sorts of names, they are treated with no respect, yet their husbands demand sex after treating them like carpets, and walking all over them.

I remind men never to trample on your wives; after all, women were not made out of feet so should not be treated that way. Like men, women are temples of the Holy Spirit, not balls for kicking around. A house should never turn into a boxing ring, as practiced in some families, especially among drunken families from various communities. Sadly, many women are bruised; battered and abused. Domestic abuse is a sin before God. Wife beating is an embarrassing and humiliating experience for a woman, and a disgrace to any man. Some men will go to the extent of verbal abuse, calling their wives "prostitutes" and other such derogatory names. Such men are boastful, oppressive, violent, arrogant and unappreciative.

Domestic violence is criminal in nature. In fact, it is a demonic spirit that should be fought in prayer. As a man, if you are ever tempted to abuse your wife, think for a minute. This battered woman is a mother (or will be one day) and at the same time a daughter, and someone's sister. Besides that she's the daugther of the most High God. She deserves respect and love.

I once read an article about a Muslim man who quoted the Qur'an saying that "a woman who disobeys her husband is entitled to admonishment and physical punishment as a last resort, until she returns to obedience." The author continued to say that, "women are to blame for their cruel treatment from men." This is unacceptable. A woman is not a punching bag. It doesn't matter what she has done wrong. Thank God, we have a God who loves us and has made us His temple. If we are His temples, we deserve to be treated special. How can anyone raise a hand to beat God's temple? Hitting a woman is like hitting God.

As a husband you should nurture, cherish, love and accept your wife just the way she is. Men who seek to have power over women should accept that their desire is wrong. And rather than waste time justifying this mistake they should work to develop Godly desires, and yield their hearts to be transformed by God. Many womenare at risk of being physically abused, if they are seen by their husbands to be questioning his autority. for example, if they happen to enquire about where their husbands have been, or how he spends the family income. This is not right. A godly and sensible man does not beat a woman; not for this reason, or any other. Some men have an archaic view that it is normal for a woman to be disadvantaged and supressed. Gone are the days when women were treated like children who are disciplined with slaps and sticks. We are privileged to live in a modern world where a woman expects companionship, affection, and support from her husband; not fighting and abuse. Thomas Aquinas, the 13th century priest, philosopher and theologian said, "He who achieves power by violence does not truly become lord or master." Also Martin Luther King, Jr. said, "Returning violence for violence multiplies violence, adding deeper darkness to a night already devoid of stars."

Praise be to Jesus who came to liberate mankind; by dying on the cross and breaking the chains of bondage. This freedom belongs to men and women alike. God has given us love, and love will conqueror all things. hitting and abusing your spouse will never bring about the change you seek. The most effective way to influence a woman behaviour is to show her love. Eventually, with time you will see a big difference in your marriage; little by little things will change.

A man who is tempted to beat his wife should find alternative strategies for dealing with these urges. For example, he could drive to a riends house to cool off, or seek counsel from his pastor, a friend or someone in a position to give good advice. As I mentined before, a wife is the weaker vessel who should be handled with care and not violence. She desires and needs protection, provision and cherishing. She is not a doormat or a second-class citizen but rather a support and helper to her husband.

Serve

A good father is a servant called to serve his family (Matthew 20:28). Jesus came to serve, not to control. Don't try to control your wife and children, but serve them. Controllong behaviour can take the form of decrees, regulations, threats and laws. "Don't do this, do that..." Husbands should set an example of service. This will inspire and encourage their families to serve each other, as demonstrated (Matthew 23:11-12). Whatever you do, do it unto the lord, with a heart of service.

It is God's will that we serve; it's not degrading to be modest and lowly in mind, to humble yourself and serve your family and others. This is God's way of leading you to heaven (John 12:26, 1 Peter 5:5-6). Your future depends on how open your heart is to serving others.

Jesus promises that if you serve Him, He will always be with you. As you serve God and others, His presence will always be with you. He also says He will honour you. This means the Lord himself will bestow honour on you; He will reward you because you serve Christ. Men, be servants in your household and you will reap a harvest; don't allow your ego to rule you but let the love of God rule you.

Protection

"Husbands, love your wives, as Christ loved the church and gave Himself up for her, that He might sanctify her, having cleansed her by the washing of water with the word, so that He might present the church to Himself in splendor, without spot or wrinkle or any such thing, that she might be holy and without blemish." Ephesians 5:25-26

According to the verse above, leadership takes special responsibility for protection and provision in the family. In the words "gave himself up for her," we hear the saving sacrifice of Jesus Christ. When Christ gave Himself up for us, He took our place. He bore our sins (1 Peter 2:24) and became a curse for us (Galatians 3:13) and died for us (Romans 5:8); and because of all this we are reconciled to God and saved from His wrath. Romans 5:10 says: "If while we were enemies we were reconciled to God by the death of His Son, much more, now that we are reconciled, shall we be saved by His life." Romans 5:10.

If there ever was an example of leadership this is it. God used initiative to protect His bride. So when Paul calls a husband to be the head of his wife by loving like Christ, it means the husband should protect the wife at all costs.

ROLES OF A WIFE

Submission

The woman is instructed in the Bible to submit thoughtfully and wisely to the leadership of her husband. Consider these words of Christ: "My Father is greater than I" John 14:28. Yet He also said, "I and My Father are one" John 10:30. Jesus came to earth to carry out the will and plan of the Father. Although He was equal to the Father, He submitted Himself to the Father's leading. This relationship within the Godhead is the pattern that provides a background for understanding heaven's pattern for marriage.

To submit means to bend, give up, give in, and agree.

You cannot have two heads. If God has called your husband as the senior pastor, please allow him lead. Don't be at loggerheads with him. There are wives who are 'strong' and hate to submit; some would prefer to fight their husbands than to submit and show honour graciously.

Stay humble. Humility will release great grace to you, and cause God to extend to you His unlimited favour and grace. As you submit in humility and in submission there is great authority. Not only will God give you more grace, He will also give you more authority over the enemy. When you are humble, God makes it His responsibility to uphold you (Psalms 41:12).

I know of a church in Uganda where the pastor and his wife fought over the church until the congregation split into two. The man took some members with him and the wife took the rest. When a woman submits to her husband, she receives a covering; and enjoys the benefits of being blessed and protected. In this story the pastor's wife missed those benefits because she did not allow her husband to lead.

You cannot bewitch a man into submission. I read a story of a woman who boasted of bewitching her husband into submission. When she quarrelled with her husband, she told him that she suspected the charm she had used to soften him for the past five years had lost its potency and threatened to contact another witch to give her stronger charms to soften him again. This angered the man, who threw her out of his house with all her property, saying he could not live with a witch. He threatened to strangle her if she came near him again.

"Wives, submit yourselves unto your own husbands, as unto the Lord." Ephesians 5:22

"Wives, likewise, be submissive to your own husbands, that even if some do not obey the word, they, without a word, may be won by the conduct of their wives, when they observe your chaste conduct accompanied by fear." 1 Peter 3:1

Admonish the young women . . . to be . . . obedient to their own husbands. Timothy 2:4-5

There are also wives who encourage their husbands to abdicate fruitful ministerial slots in churches to go and start new churches. But churches founded on sinister motives are doomed to failure.

Some wives can be verbally abusive, calling their husbands fools and other names to put them down. This behaviour is not pleasing to God, and the question I would ask such a women is; if you're so smart, why did you marry a fool in the first place. If a woman believes that a man is a fool, she should refrain committing herself to him in marriage. I pray that the fear of the Lord be with us, because it is the fear of the God that helps us to exercise self-control and humility.

"Submitting yourselves one to another in the fear of God." Ephesians 5:21

If God happens to call a wife to be the senior pastor of a church, her husband should support her, and stand with her. However, this doesn't mean that as a wife she should not submit to her husband. *Whether at church or home, honour, revere and respect your man.* Peter and I consult each other when making important decisions, or major purchases. We do it more out of respect than to get permission.

"...and the wife see that she reverence her." Ephesians 5:33

If given an opportunity to talk anywhere, acknowledge your husband; talk about him in a godly way and praise him. Even if you are more spiritual or intellectual than your husband, you will be wise to encourage him and make him feel like a king. Every man needs the approval and encouragement of his wife. By doing thiss you will end up disarming the spirit of competition and strife. This same principle applies to husbands who are more spiritual than their wives.

Woman, although it may be challenging at time, learn to be submissive to your husband. A wife's submission should not be misunderstood to mean that she loses her right to have and express her own opinions. A woman should always be given the freedom to voice her godly views.

Thank God we are believers; we have the privilege of putting our trust in God concerning our partners, we have this advantage over people of the world. When a wife rebels against her God-given man, she rebels against God who created order and authority. Most of us women rebel for selfish reasons, not scriptural ones. For example, if you want to go to a conference, do not say to yourself 'I will go even if I don't inform my husband of where I am. After all I'm going to a godly meeting.'

Even women in church struggle. When the message 'gets to us,' we take it out on the messenger. We don't want to hear any message about submission through the preacher oranyone else. The truth is you'll keep going from one bad situation to another, until you finally learn to submit to your husband. God placed you under the authority of your husband; and He's interested in your level of submission and is working on you so that you will improve it. He's preparing you for battle! If you can't follow instruction, you will be an easy target for the enemy. As a woman of God I advice you to put aside your personal agenda, and submit to your husband. God will then honor and promote you!

How do I deal with a non-believing partner?

How can you submit to a husband who is not a Christian? You can not submit to him spiritually, of course, unless he is submitted to Christ. Nor can you submit if he requires you to commit some sin, since your submission to Christ takes precedence over your submission to any human being. However, submission to a non saved spouse is still required as long as you are not being made to sin.

Respect

Woman, if you are married, stay in your position so as to bring God's glory to your home. Respect that man and love him the way he is. In her book, Dr. Claudette Anderson Copeland says, "Love is not for the lazy." It is birthed in the heart by the miracle of grace." Love and respect go together. Every man loves to be respected, regardless of his income bracket. Even if he comes from a poor background; he deserves respect because a husband's most basic need is for respect and intimacy from his wife.

Respect, according to the late Pastor Bimbo, is "The very foundation of a successful marriage. It involves caring about the other person's best interest and not pushing only for selfish gain." Mutual respect is of paramount importance for the success of any marriage. If you don't respect your husband, it will be hard submitting to him, and of course, he will not love you as he should. You might say, "Well, for me to submit, he has to first love me." But God expects you to play your role as a woman regardlss how your husband measures up to his duties. Why wait for him to show you love, when you can sow seeds of love into your marriage? Go ahead and respect him because your reward is in heaven and as you do the right thing, you may be suprised how quickly your husband changes his behaviour.

A woman was not created to compete with her husband but to complete him. Women who choose to apply the word of God to their marriage shall be powerful in Him. The greatness that God gave us as women increases as we put His word into action. Rather than fight for power, we need to take our rightful place, as partners to our husbands.

I know of a married sister, mightily used of God, but who always pushed to have her way in every situation that required a choice in the home. I doubt that there are many men who would like that. Besides, it's not biblical. This sister was not submissive, and was known to shout at her husband in front of their children, and their friends. After any argument, she would throw his clothes out, slap him and walk out on him to meet with her friends. How terrible! Finally, I was told this man refused to tolerate his wifes behaviour any longer, and walked out never to return.

Women, when you honour your husband, it glorifies God, by demonstrating your obedience to His order. Resist any temptation to compete. You should not fear your husband but must show him respect, as the Bible instructs. The fear of man is a snare before God and perfect love casts out fear. Gone are the days when women are bound by tradition. Women were not allowed to minister or even speak in times past. God gave you a mouth to praise Him and preach the gospel of the Kingdom of heaven. Yes, God has called you, but be humble. God has set us free but we need to be careful not to go to the extreme of insubordination. Which will cause us to miss out on what He intended us to be. It is a sin for women to rule over men. If you have done it, I urge you to humble yourself before God and repent. If you as a woman happen to be the breadwinner it doesn't change the order of God; therefore you are still required to submit. Even if you are the one who bought the house you both live in, that does not make you more important than your husband. The way up is to go downward, and become lowly in humility. Satan was thrown out of heaven due to pride. Pride is responsible for more deaths than cancer. But if you humble yourself, God will reward you. Do not be like the women whose tendency to demean their husbands is at "PHD" (Pull Husband Down) level. Mistreat your husband at your own peril.

There are cases where women make themselves as masters over their husbands, just like Jezebel of the Bible. A friend of mine told me a story of a lady who made her husband do all the housework including cooking, washing dishes and cleaning the house. This was on top of his role as breadwinner. To make matters worse, she would never go out with him, but preferred to go with friends.

In all this time, the man continued to give financial support every week for her personal needs. She wasn't grateful but continued to mistreat him, forgetting she was created to be a helper, and not a master. In the end, the marriage ended in divorce. Marriages like this invariably do.

Helper

"And the Lord God said, "It is not good that man should be alone; I will make him a helper comparable to him." Genesis 2:18.

Helper, love your husband. This will bring your

relationship to another level. Everyday endeavour to look beyond his weakness; see him through the eyes of Christ. His first need is your love and companionship. "…that they admonish the young women to love their husbands, and to love their children." (Titus 2:4). Not only are you help to love your husband but also help him by praying for him, encouraging and supporting his business and ministry. One of the duties of the Holy Spirit is to help us. "And I will pray to the Father, and He will give you another Helper, that He may abide with you forever…" (John 14:16). The Holy Spirit is always present with us 24/7 to empower and strengthen us. That is the role we must play in our spouses lives.

The reason why God made women the helper and companion to their husbands man is because Adam could not find a creature corresponding to himself among the animals he was commissioned to name. As a Christian wife, you should see yourself as a spiritual companion. You and your husband are making a spiritual journey through life together, walking hand in hand as children of God, towards the wonderful eternity with God that awaits you.

"…because the Lord has been witness between you and the wife of your youth, with whom you have dealt treacherously; yet she is your companion and your wife by covenant. Malachi 2:14

It should be the priority of every woman to help her husband. I heard of a lady who got married to a wonderful but less educated young man. Rather than look down on him, she encouraged him to go back and study. She paid his school fees and today he is a graduate with a very good job. This wife helped her husband to aim higher. Thankfully, this man did not feel intimidated or inferior to his wife's success, but chose to look beyond that. Men who find themselves in a situation where their wives are relatively more successful in their careers, should take this as an example.

Meet his sexual needs

A woman must help her husband to avoid fornication. Are you really helping? In the garden of paradise where it all began, Adam and Eve shared a wonderful intimacy; "They were both naked, the man and his wife, and were not ashamed" (Gen. 2:25). Intimacy and mutual physical fulfillment, therefore, have always been part of the husband-wife relationship. Wives, it is your duty to meet your husbands' sexual desires, do not deny your husband what he needs. You cannot have a headache all the time!

A husband and wife who maintain intimacy are helping to protect each other from a sexually obsessed society. They protect their own faithfulness, and their health.

There's no better time to start than now if you have not been treating your spouse the way you should. Wake up, the devil is like a roaring lion looking for someone to devour (1 Peter 5:8). We shall look at this topic in detail in the coming chapters.

Childbearing
"...you shall bring forth children..." Genesis 3:16

To "bear children" does not simply mean to bring them into the world. It means to train them and nurture them. Can I also encourage husbands to share in the labour of raising children. It will help you to appreciate your wife more.

"... just as a nursing mother cherishes her own children." 1 Thessalonians 2:7

Look at what Paul said to the Thessalonian church about how a mother should look after her child. You are to cherish your children. The word "cherish" means to protect or tend (a children, plant, etc.) lovingly; it also means to cling to. Love your children; protect them from the evil of this world.

I believe that all parents will agree with me when I say that having children and raising them up is not easy. It is hard work and it takes the grace of God. To conceive them may be relatively easy, but when it comes to raising, training, and disciplining them – that is another story altogether. Being a parent is such a great joy. The amount of fulfillment and laughter it brings into your life, coupled with the sense of purpose and meaning is so great. However, on a less exciting note, the weight of responsibility that comes with parenthood; the pain of child birth, the recognisable loss of freedom, the sleepless nights, the alteration of career prospects, and the dependence on husbands (for wives in some cases) is not always easy. The best way to handle this pressure is to follow the plan of God concerning raising your children, and be guided by the best teacher - the Holy Spirit.

As a mother you are to cook, clean, bake, care for your children and attend to the innumerable affairs of a busy household. It has been said, "The training and toil of motherhood will not gain you acclaim in this world, but it will in the next!" In my book "Mum and dad wake up" I go into more detail on parenting.

Manage household

Manage your home wisely, let every bit be organised. Your home should reflect the wholeness and beauty of God's presence in your heart. You have been anointed to bring uniqueness in your home, therefore you are to make a difference in your home. It has been said,

"HUMANITY MOVES BETWEEN THE TWO POLES NAMELY, "SIMPLICITY" AND "COMPLEXITY."
-PAUL TOURNIER-

"Home is where the heart is." Let God's presence fill your home. Let people feel peace when they come to your house. Make your house a blessing. Dedicate your home to God. It should be a place where you nurture life. If you are to manage your family affairs learn to be good managers (Tim.5:14).

"…that they admonish the young women to love their husbands, to love their children, to be discreet, chaste, homemakers, good, obedient to their own husbands…" Titus 2:5

You are to be a worker "keeper at home." The word "keeper" means a worker. As a woman it means your career is in the home. One of the hardest things I had to learn as a wife, was to be satisfied with realising that my ministry is primarily in the home. I believe many wives today would agree with me.

Many married women today, even Christian ladies, have placed the pursuit of a career above home making. This is perilous to the God-ordained family structure. As women, home making should be our first priority. It is a full time job. You are to take care of your husband. Your career is to make your husband a success. Educate your children; raise them in a godly way. Motherhood is a career that demands all your focus and energy. Be a vessel of the grace of God to your children. Read my book *"Woman You Are Great."* You will need to strike a balance, and this book will advise you on how to do that effectively.

Chapter 11

KEEPING YOUR LOVE TANK FULL

I have heard a story of a woman who woke up one night to find that her husband wasn't in bed beside her. She found him in the kitchen looking very serious. So she asked, "What's going on?" He replied, "Remember in high school when your dad caught us kissing and said if I didn't marry you immediately, he'd make sure I was jailed for 20 years? Well, I'm sitting here thinking I would have gotten out of jail today!"

A strong marriage means falling in love over and over again, with the same person! You walk through the challenges together and still maintain your love for one another.

Here are some secrets to help you keep your love tank full, so that you can enjoy your marriage. They are simple and practical:

1. RELATIONSHIP WITH GOOD

Psalm 127:1 tells us that "Unless the Lord builds the house, they labour in vain who build it; unless the Lord guards the city the watchman stays awake in vain." Believe me or not, if you don't allow God into your marriage you cannot build it with wisdom. Because wisdom comes from Him. That is why there are many couples who are not building their homes but tearing them down. God will give you a design for building your marriage. *"By wisdom a house is built, and through understanding it is established; by knowledge its rooms are filled with all kinds of precious and pleasing treasures."* Proverbs 24:3-4

God tells us that there are three things we need if we are going to build: wisdom, understanding, and knowledge. God's Word gives us these three things. He is the author of marriage, and therefore His principles do work. Please take the time to pray and ask God for the grace to be the kind of wife or husband who can truly build a home according to God's design. Pray for faithfulness, humility, and the desire to obey God day after day, despite the circumstances or the responses of your spouse, or those around you. When storms come, God will see you through when you make Him the third party in your relationship. God will give you wisdom to lead your family. And when you invite Him into your marriage, everything will fall in place. One step at a time, A failure to invite Him in will result in inevitable choas.

2. PRAY TOGETHER

Pray and read the Bible together and ask God to give you more love for each other. Romans 5:5 tell us that *"Hope doesn't disappoint but the love of God has been poured out in our hearts…"* One thing that I have observed over time is that most couples don't pray together. But it is prayer that will bring joy, peace, etc, into our homes. Some people don't pray because they don't believe in themselves and would prefer. They prefer their pastors and leaders to pray for them. God has called us all to have fellowship with Him, everyday. If a man prays for his children, it's better than giving them millions of dollars. Your brother or sister, children and spouse are in need of your prayers. One of the ways I have been able to maintain a healthy relationship with my husband Peter, is through praying, studying God's word and discussing the word together.

"Again I say to you that if two of you agree on earth concerning anything that they ask, it will be done for them by My Father in heaven. For where two or three are gathered together in My name, I am there in the midst of them." Mathew 18:19

Your relationship is strengthened when you pray together. You will accomplish much more than you thought was possible. According to the familiar adage, 'A couple that prays together surely will stay together.' It has been said about love that "it is a metaphor taken from a number of musical instruments set to the same key, and playing the same tune: this means a perfect agreement of the hearts, desires, wishes, and voices, of two or more persons praying to God. It also intimates that as a number of musical instruments, skillfully played, in a good concert, are pleasing to the ears of men, so a number of persons united together in warm, earnest, cordial prayer, is highly pleasing in the sight and ears of the Lord." Praying together is so important that the devil will try everything to stop you from doing it. He will tell you, "You are tired; why pray with your spouse; pray tomorrow." When tomorrow comes, he will give you another excuse, "You can pray alone, God will hear your prayers." Sometimes Jesus prayed alone, other times he prayed with the disciples.

"And when He had sent the multitudes away, He went up on the mountain by Himself to pray. Now when evening came, He was alone there. But the boat was now in the middle of the sea, tossed by the waves, for the wind was contrary. Now in the fourth watch of the night Jesus went to them, walking on the sea." Mathew 14:23-26

Praying together as a couple will strengthen your relationship. Your spouse and children may be giving you problems but continue praying until you see the manifestatin of your prayers.

The devil's plan is to separate you from your partner, and cause a divorce. Moreso, when you are called to work together towards a common goal, to pray together. Satan knows the power of agreement (Mathew 18:19).

Happily married?

Even if you are happily married and settled, good, but that's not the end of the story. God expects you to stand and help those who are struggling in their marriages. Pray for them, and support them. By doing this you will sow good seeds for your own relationship.

"Then Joshua commanded the officers of the people, saying, pass through the host, and command the people, saying, Prepare you victuals; for within three days ye shall pass over this Jordan, to go in to possess the land, which the LORD your God giveth you to possess it. And to the Reubenites, and to the Gadites, and to half the tribe of Manasseh, spake Joshua, saying, remember the word which Moses the servant of the LORD commanded you, saying, the LORD your God hath given you rest, and hath given you this land. Your wives, your little ones, and your cattle,

shall remain in the land which Moses gave you on this side Jordan; but ye shall pass before your brethren armed, all the mighty men of valour, and help them; until the LORD have given your brethren rest, as He hath given you, and they also have possessed the land which the LORD your God giveth them: then ye shall return unto the land of your possession, and enjoy it, which Moses the LORD'S servant gave you on this side Jordan toward the sun rising." Joshua 1:10-15

From this example, Joshua told the Reubenities, the Gadites and the half-tribe of Manasseh to remember the command that Moses the servant of the Lord had given them. God had given them rest, and had granted them their land. He had given them Jordan; Joshua told them that their wives, children and livestock would stay in Jordan, but all their fighting men were to be fully armed and had to cross over ahead of their brothers. He commanded them to help their brother until the Lord would give them rest, as He had done for them (Reubanities the Gadites), and until they too would take possession of the land that the Lord their God was giving them. You cannot just settle in your own marriage, business, etc; then enjoy life and completely forget other marriages that are struggling. Pray for them because they want to experience the peace, prosperity and success you have. And God has helped you to prosper so that you can help someone else in need.

Joshua instructed that after the men of Israel had fought, and helped their brothers, they were free to go back to occupy their own land, which Moses the servant of the Lord had given them, in the east of the Jordan toward the sunrise. Thank God they obeyed. Let's look at how they responded.

"And they answered Joshua, saying, all that thou commandest us we will do, and whithersoever thou sendest us, we will go. According as we hearkened unto Moses in all things, so will we hearken unto thee: only the LORD thy God be with thee, as he was with Moses. Whosoever he be that doth rebel against thy commandment, and will not hearken unto thy words in all that thou commandest him, he shall be put to death: only be strong and of a good courage." Joshua 1:16-18

Get out of your comfort zone and pray for others, we are fighting the same devil everywhere; and he can knock at your own door anytime. We are in a battle; if you don't pray for others, what if one day the trouble they face turns up at your own home? What will you do? You need other people's prayers much as they need yours. The prayer and support of others will help you to keeo your own love tank full.

3. REAL LOVE

Refill your love tank regularly. It's impossible to escape marital stress but you can control it by taking occasional breaks from the daily grind. Take walks together, go out for lunch or tea, do whatever it takes to reconnect with your spouse. And let your family know that you're taking time out. If your children are old enough to understnad, let them know.

Even if your needs are not being met in your marriage, love and honour your spouse, regardless. Husbands love your wives as Christ loved the church. Everyday tell your wife that you love her. Shower her with affection and make her feel cherished and special - women need that!

Some people genuinely have a problem with showing love; sometimes because they were not loved when they were young. They may have been rejected and abused. A person with such a history will find it difficult to express to themselves and others. But this should not be an excuse, not to love, if you come from a troubled background there's hope for you. No matter what your problem, you are at liberty to ask the Holy Spirit to teach you how to love (Romans 5:5).

How do you respond to a spouse who has issues with showing love? The answer is to show them love. Love conquers all things! Don't give up. Ask God to fill you with an abundance of love, and pray for your spouse.

4. SPECIAL TIME

After creating heaven and earth, God rested on the seventh day. If God rested, you also need to do so. Include holidays together into you plans. Go away as a couple and get refreshed. Take some quality time to work on your marriage. This gives you the opportunity to catch up on the issues in your marriage. In this twenty first century, where time is very limited, many things are competing for our time, the internet, television, computer games, friends, family, mail and television, etc. We need to use our time wisely. spend time getting to know each other better. What are your spouse's interests? Do they enjoy watching movies, playing football, etc? What perfumes do they like? Do they enjoy listening to music? If so, what genre do they listen to? These are things you need to understand about your partner.

Some newly-wed couples don't make time for each other after the honey moon is over. Create time at home for you and your partner to talk about your love for each other. Review your wedding albums and videos, repeat your wedding vows. to one another.

"When a man hath taken a new wife, he shall not go out to war, neither shall he be charged with any

business: but he shall be free at home one year, and shall cheer up his wife which he hath taken." Deuteronomy 24:5

"It is a sign between me and the children of Israel for ever: for in six days the LORD made heaven and earth, and on the seventh day He rested, and was refreshed." Exodus 31:17

Give each other undivided attention. Go out on dates, take holidays, have evening walks, and enjoy each other. You need to take time away from everything, including your kids. "You must never find the time for anything. If you want time you must make it" Buxton.

You don't have to save huge amounts of money to go away. You can decide to go to a beach, or have a picnic. If you have children, arrange for someone to baby-sit. My husband Peter always surprises me. One day he took me to a very posh hotel in Israel where we had a good time. By the time we came back home, we were both refreshed and stress free. And our love had been elevated to a new level.

People spend a lot of time listening to music and watching television. They spend less time reading God's word. They think that success in life has to do with professional achievement, financial success, and family solidarity. God comes before all of those things.

He always wants first place in your life.
"As every thread of gold is valuable, so is every minute of time." John Mason

Be balanced. Use your time wisely. Don't make your marriage suffer as a result of your career and church programmes. Set your priorities right. Make a programme for the day. Say no to some things in order to spend time with your mate. Aim to come immediately after work, or else you may find your spouse asleep or too tired to even listen to you discuss your day. Switch off your house phone occasionally so that you have time with your family.

Both husbands and wives are co-workers in God's kingdom; you are to help each other fulfill your God-given destinies. Talk about your marriage, future plans, etc. By doing this, you will become increasingly fulfilled and happy.

Some of us give far too much time to our friends and fellow church members. When you get entangled in other people's lives, you lose focus on your God, and your marriage suffers because you are everything to every body. Please understand me, I am not against serving God or even praying for people, but we need to strike a balance. Otherwise you will fail to get time for your own family and your God. Being with friends is not bad but if it is over done, it has the potential to encourage unfruitful behaviur, which could have a detrimental impact on your relationship. This problem is often more common among women. My advice is to find alternative ways to keep yourself occupied. Consider writing a book or helping the needy, become a member of a club or society; or simply spend some quality time with your family. These are all ways in which you can be constructively busy. Gossip is a sin, and it can break our fellowship with God. There are some people who call themselves God's prayer warriors but are rather avid gossips. God is interested in our character, and is unimpressed with gossiping behaviour.

I read about a family that had problems in their marriage. They decided to go away on a holiday to have quality time. During their time away, the husband and wife had an argument, and the husband leaped from the balcony of the hotel with his children in his arms in an apparent suicide attempt. His six-year old son was killed and the daughter aged two was seriously injured in the fall. This was a young family ripped apart by the devil. The holiday ended in a tragedy. The devil came to kill steal and destroy. It seems the man was depressed. As Christians, we need to put our burdens before the Lord, and not try to handle when we find that we cannot manage. When you go away for your quality time together focus on building your relationship.

Allow your inner child to surface; play hide-and-seek and enjoy one another. Every year that goes by can never be re-lived; therefore play with your mate and seize every opportunity to develop fun and memorable experiences together.

"There is a time for everything, and a season for every activity under heaven." Ecclesiastes 3:1

Celebrate special occasions, like birthdays and wedding anniversaries. I read about a couple in Dallas, Texas who were celebrating their 10th wedding anniversary. The wife ordered a life–size cake, a replica of herself, and it was 1.5m high (5ft) and weighed 180 Kg (400lb). It contained 200 eggs and 7.5litres of amaretto. It was so big that it took four men to carry it to the venue. She said, "Growing up, I always wanted a doll made in my likeness, I wanted a life-size cake made in my resemblance as I would look on my wedding day." Wow! What an interesting story. It demonstrates how creative you can be when you put your mind to it. Let your creative juice flow from your heart, and make sure what you do is meaningful and relevant to your relationship.

5. ROMANTIC GETAWAYS

I used to be very bitter when my husband forgot about my birthday. I would wait until his birthday just to give him a taste of his own medicine. But one day after praying, the Holy Spirit said to me, "Jo, humble yourself! Why are you always complaining and planning revenge? That's not godly. I want you to go and organise Peter a surprise birthday, look for a posh hotel and take him there" I replied, "But Lord that's so expensive." He said to me, "Well, he deserves the best, I died for him and I love him as my son; go ahead, I will provide." I couldn't believe it. When I took the first step of calling and booking the hotel, the Lord Jesus took the second step the following day by blessing me with enough money for the party. God is a wonderful and loving Father.

I gave my husband a surprise birthday party as instructed by the Lord in an expensive five star hotel. I packed his clothes and gave them to my friend Susan to take them to the hotel. At the end of a marriage conference that we had organised, I told my husband that we had been invited to a couple's dinner. When we arrived at the hotel, we were welcomed by the receptionist who showed us our room. As I opened the door, my husband was startled and wide-eyed, as I began to sing, "Happy Birthday to you…" Oh! You should have seen him. His eyes became wet, he ran short of words, he hugged and kissed me; we talked about our love for each other. The rest is history. That was the beginning of another romantic journey! Because I obeyed God, I started seeing His favor in my life as never before. My husband became so loving, caring, understanding, humble and sweet. Of course he still has weaknesses but I choose to look at his strengths. Our family became more joyful, and God opened up doors for me to minister. The testimonies are too many to mention but the message is clear, obedience is better than sacrifice. My fellow sisters and brothers in Christ, don't wait for your partner to do something good for you. Go ahead and do it for them; it will be so rewarding. Ask your spouse, "what can I do to make you happy?"

Can you believe that what I did challenged him so much that on Valentine's Day he surprised me with a weekend at a posh hotel outside London? It was quiet and romantic. He organised the next outing with friends without my knowledge. Wow! The place was gorgeous. Peter later took me to Israel, where my love for him just exploded. It pays off to go on romantic getaways together. You don't have to be rich to do fun and memorable activities together. You could simply go for a cup of coffee in a restaurant or have a picnic in a nice park.

6. BE CONSISTENT

When you get married, be careful of what you permit in the beginning, because it will come to be expected. For example, if you are going to have a pet name for each other, be prepared to keep doing it. When you change, your partner will think that something is wrong, or your love for them is reducing. Decide now what you can live with later.

7. COOKING

Nowadays it is not common for some women not to cook. Men love women who cook. After a long day, most men will expect to find a lovely meal awaiting them. "The way to a man's heart is through his stomach," and "a hungry man is an angry man." Women, you will do well to practice preparing lovely meals for the special man in your life. And husbands, surprise your wife by making her a cup of tea, or even preparing a meal once in a while.

"So the king and Haman came to banquet with Esther the queen. And the king said again unto Esther on the second day at the banquet of wine, what is thy petition, Queen Esther? And it shall be granted thee: and what is thy request? And it shall be performed, even to the half of the kingdom." Esther 7:1-3

The king had come to have a meal with Esther and it gave her the opportunity to share her heart. Eating together as a family is important, and a godly practice. We shouldn't ignore it's importance. When families can get to know what has been happening to each other in the day; it's a good time for fellowship and bonding. "There's no sight on earth more appealing than the sight of a woman making dinner for someone she loves" Thomas Wolfe.

8. GIVE GIFTS

Buy special gifts for each other. Remember a gift doesn't buy love. Give when it's necessary, but not to impress, or as a substitute for genuine and consistent love. I give my husband gifts not to favour me but because I love him.

Do not grow weary in doing good, for in due season you shall reap, if you do not give up (Galatians 6: 9). Your reward is here on earth and in heaven. God gave us Jesus Christ and was rewarded with the hearts of men and women, even over two thousand years later. Give at all times, and not just when the sales are on.

- Gifts express romance
- Gifts show that "I was thinking about you."
- Songs of Solomon in the Bible demonstrates the

value of giving gifts, where the author promises to give his woman earrings.

• Jesus bought your spouse at a high price, so why not buy them the best?

Keep your word

When you keep your promises to your spouse, it shows that you honour them. If you have difficulty fulfilling your promise, explain why you failed or else you will cause your partner to loose trust for you. Sow seeds constantly into your relationship as and when the Lord leads you. You are not buying God, but rather you are activating the laws of reaping and sowing. And the Bible advises us that 'whatsoever a man sows that shall he also reap (Galatians 6:7). Look at Cornelius. God told him "I have seen your prayers and you're giving." So shall it be with you as you continue to give gifts, sowing all kinds of good seeds in your partner's life. God will see your giving, and you shall be rewarded.

9. APPRECIATION:

There is no one who doesn't want to be appreciated. If you send a child to do something, and offer your thanks after, they will want to do more for you. However, if you don't show any appreciation, they may try to rebel. Appreciating what a child does excites, motivates and encourages them. The same principle applies to us adults. When we feel appreciated, we are motivated to do more. Make an effort to show you partner appreciation.

Learn to say thank you for the small and big things they do. Husbands tell your wife "I appreciate you for being the mother of my children" and wive, tell your husbands "Thank you for marrying me, for being there for me always." Say thank you when she irons your shirts, when he opens a door for you. Exercise Kingdom manners. Even in incidents where a stranger helps you out in some way; thank them for it. If someone gives you the right of way as you are driving, wave at them. Some people will give you a cold, unappreciative stare after you have given them the right of way to drive off in front of you. It has been said that, "We are so often caught up in our destination that we forget to appreciate the journey, especially the goodness of the people we meet on the way. Appreciation is a wonderful feeling, don't overlook it." Don't look for the worst; learn to look for the best in each other. Be affirming. It takes 12 compliments to neutralize one criticism. Your partner won't know how wonderful they are unless you tell them!

10. PHYSICAL TOUCH

This is another way of communicating love. According to research, being hugged, held and kissed developed a healthier emotional life. *"Then the little children were brought to Him that He might put His hands on them and pray, but the disciples rebuked them."* Matthew 19:13-14

Hold each other often. Let the world see that you love each other, and make the devil envious. Psychologists say that an average woman needs eight meaningful touches a day, to live a normal life. Pastors, sit with your wives. Don't leave them to sit at the back in the church. Wink at your partner, gently hold each other's hands. Connecting in this this way on a physical level, helps to develop and maintain an intimate bond that will strengthen your marriage.

11. BELIEVE IN EACH OTHER

Believe in each other's vision and plans. God brought you together to support each other. You are for him; she is for you. A divided house cannot stand (Matthew 12:25). It's your duty as a couple to see that you make your marriage a success and fulfill God's will and purpose for your lives. Talk about one another positively in the presence of other people; let them know that you believe in each other.

12. ACQUIRE KNOWLEDGE

One of the ways to make your love tank full is to acquire more knowledge from experienced people. Go for seminars, workshops and read books. Put what you learn into practice. If you're not informed you are deformed. Learning should only stop when you're dead. Good leaders are always readers. You're a leader in your home, so go ahead and read about subjects that you think will help i.e. marriage, children, financial management, etc. There is a saying that often rings true, that *"If you want to hide something from a fool, put it in a book."* What did God say to Hosea? "My people perish because of lack of knowledge." When you are well informed, the devil will fight you but he will not prevail.

When you listen to other people's testimonies, you will discover that what you are going through in your marriage is also happening or has happened to some else. As I mentioned in earlier chapters, you can attend marriage seminars. I have so many testimonies of couples whose marriages have been transformed, restored and healed through hearing God's word. Here are two testimonies that were given in one of our meetings. Because of what God did for these people, they asked me to always share their testimonies so that other couples may learn from them.

"Coming to the marriage conference was a time of

refreshment in my life and marriage. I am married to a bishop and l had problems. After I had an operation on my womb, I discovered that I no longer had feelings for my husband. Through the teachings about marriage, God healed me and the following day my husband came to testify in the meeting. Glory to God!" **Pastor Rachael. Tanzania.**

Stella Nantongo, a minister in one of the churches found in the rural parts of Uganda, testified how God restored her marriage and saved her drunkard husband. With tears of joy and gratitude, she explained how she had come close to losing her marriage, which was not even legal. She said, *"After Pastor Josephine prayed for me in the previous meeting held here, I started experiencing a dramatic change in my marriage. My husband got saved and we also wedded in church. I'm now enjoying a marriage full of peace and happiness."* Praise the Lord.

Look at this wonderful woman of God. After my speech, she went home and forgave her husband. She put the advice she received into action. She is a doer of God's word. These are some of the benefits of attending meetings for couples.

13. PHYSICAL APPEARANCE

God created you to attract your suitable mate. Men are taken up by what they see and women by what they hear. Look at Song of Solomon 1:12, 4:1-7, 5:5. Work on your weight, but don't over do it. It's scientifically proven that men on the whole are not attracted to anorexic women. They like women who have a bit of flesh. Please improve on your appearance. Some ladies are care free. Even if their husbands tell them to improve on their appearance they don't care. Come on girl, have some life! Please have a teachable spirit. You might say, "I don't even have enough clothes." Well, I do understand; but even with the few you have, make sure they fit and are neat.

This may not come as a surprise to many men, but an average woman spends two years of her life gazing at the mirror. More than half of women confessed to looking at their reflections in anything with a reflection. In contrast, men devote less than half a year of their time looking at a mirror, a survey by a spectacles company showed.

When God made you, He made you beautiful. You were created in His image and He was pleased with you. So maintain your beauty. Wear nice fragrances to smell good for your mate. The Bible says perfume and incense bring joy to the heart. When you wear perfume and smell good, you bring joy to your man. I recommend you read my book titled "Woman you are great." If talks more about matters of appearance.

"Ointment and perfume rejoice the heart…" Proverbs 27:9

14. PRAISE

When was the last time your praised your spouse? Or when you received praise from them? Do you acknowledge each others compliments? Women, if your husband says "I love your hair do," or "I love the way you smile." Do you reply, "Oh, no, are you sure?" Yes, he means it! How do you feel when someone tells you, "You look beautiful?" "Your nails look pretty". Of course you feel good.

As you sow words of praise, you will both feel special to one another. King Solomon said, *Proverbs 15:4 "A soothing tongue is a tree of life."* Everyone loves to be praised and your mate is no exception.

William James wrote, "The deepest principal in human nature is the craving to be appreciated." Mark Twain said, "I can live for two months on a good compliment."
We praise our friends, and colleagues, yet sometimes neglect our homes where praise ought to be applied

liberally. Praise means to give value, to lift up, to extol, to magnify, and to honor, to commend or applaud. If you had given up because of the disappointments you have faced in your marriage I want to encourage you to start again. Be like Christ. He doesn't look at our weakness but at our strengths. Gideon, Moses and many others in the Bible are proof of what I am saying. The more you praise your mate, the more secure your mate will feel. An encouraging word can help lighten the load and lift your partner's spirits.

Solomon, the wisest king on earth said, "An anxious heart weighs a man down but a kind word cheers him up." Nagging is not the solution. Showing genuine respect and giving sincere praise, is a solution. As I mentioned before, it is a good idea to name pet names. Have pet names for each other. In Song of Solomon 1:9, the man uses "Darling", 1:13 the woman uses "My lover" 1 Peter 3:16; and Sarah called Abraham Lord, in honour and respect of him.

Harsh words, mood swings and bad attitudes will cause your man to keep away from you. Healthy words will promote your relationship. Choose what you say wisel, and let your spouse be your best friend.

Build Self-esteem

Build your spouse's self-esteem. Let your partner know how great they are. Marriage is God's workshop for self-esteem building. Part of God's plan for marriage is for you to help your spouse become all that he or she was intended to be. While that may sound like a big job, all it takes is letting your mate know that you accept them and are committed to meeting their needs. Developing and building self esteem is, therefore, one of the most important and valuable things you could ever do for yourself, your partner, your children and others.

Every parent has the task of boost their children's confidence. You need to let them know how great they are so that they do not seek somebody else's approval. My husband and I give our teenage children the reassurance they need to believe in themselves. They are confident and proud of themselves in the Lord. I have always told my boys that they are handsome and recently, my son Derrick came up to me and said, "Mum, I surely am handsome! As I walk out there, all the girls look at me." This sent us bursting into laughter, Davis too always tells me "Mum, I don't even know my name anymore; the girls keep calling me 'Handsome,' they say I look cool, and my height is unique. Now, that is self-esteem for you. I just laugh and say "Ya man!"

Peter always tells me "Darling you can do any thing in Christ." He's such an encourager. Through him, I have been able to fulfill my assignments in writing and preaching the gospel to nations. Wow! He never stands in the way of God by discouraging me in my service God. Honey! God bless you. God intends all binding relationships to draw us closer to Him, never to become an idol that takes us away from Him. Some spouses can become a hindrance by discouraging their partners from fulfilling God's purpose in life. Others are blinded by love for each other. Their whole focus is being together and they don't sacrifice time to serve God, forgetting that they themselves can become an idol before God, if they are not careful. Exodus 20:3 says, "Thou shalt have no other gods before me."

The wellspring inside us is the place we gather the resources to give to others, and as we give to others our own self-esteem is boosted. When God is the source of this wellspring and you are complete in Him; loving your family becomes a less laborious task. Friends, I urge you to spend time in God's presence and let him teach you how to love and praise each other. Receive an impartation from the Most High that propels you above your usual perspective, 'Enlarge the place of your tent' (Isaiah 54:2), get the Lord's point of view of yourself your spouse and your children. Let Him touch your eyes so that you may see differently, and view those around you in a new way.

Don't allow your shortcomings to steal your self-esteem. Press through the issues that keep you in bondage until you touch the hem of his garment. Draw wisdom from the woman with the issue of blood (Mark 5: 25-34). She refused to allow the social leprosy of her condition to stop her from receiving her healing. Instead, she risked all she had and pressed through the crowd of her present fears, past failures and parental future rejections. Her faith stopped Jesus in his tracks. As a result, she received healing for her condition. But Jesus didn't just stop there; He spoke into her life and she was made whole (He restored her to her original state). She had an encounter with The Word Himself and her life was never the same again. Understand this friend: you need to press through and touch the hem of His garment to see your spouse, family members and friends as Jesus sees them. He sees beyond our weakness, and esteems us all highly.

Chapter 12

SEX

This topic has been neglected in the body of Christ, and because of that, many marriages have ended up in divorce. Many ministers do not feel free to discuss it because they fear being misunderstood. I myself struggled while writing about this topic. I pleaded with God for His assurance, and the Holy Spirit told me that many couples need to be educated. How will they know unless we teach them? The fear of man is a snare before God. I would rather obey God than fear mortal man. The devil is taking full advantage in this area, because the church is not talking about it. Many couples have approached me after our seminars, asking if I had a book on this topic.

Just because I am sharing knowledge about sex, doesn't mean I am not spiritual. I do fast, pray and speak in tongues. As a matter of fact, most of the things I am sharing with you have been revealed to me by the Holy Spirit. We have taught them in our "Rekindle your love" conferences and seminars and many marriages have been restored. So should I fear to help someone out there, whose marriage is dying? No way! I hate the devil. I would rather speak out in obedience to God than fear man's judgment. I would rather please my Master Jesus, than please man by keeping quiet. In the book of James 1:17 we are told, "Every good and perfect gift comes from God" Sex is a gift from God; it is healthy, exciting and enjoyable. Sex is one of the things that make marriage enjoyable. It unites you with your partner, in spirit, in body, and in mind. Sexual satisfaction is good and godly. It keeps couples calm and loving. The Bible says Adam and Eve were both naked (Gen 3:7). Adam knew his wife Eve. The word knew comes from the word *Gynocso*, a Greek word meaning intimately had sex (Genesis 4:1).

This chapter contains what I have been teaching couples every where I go, and I have seen God restore marriages as a result. What is the point of pretending that everything is ok, when our homes are dying? God created sex. I taught on these issues sorrounding sex and a Bishop's marriage was restored. Sex in their home was boring until God visited them through the teachings I delivered.

INTIMACY

Express love to each other throughout the day; don't wait until you have sex to show intimacy. Intimacy is more than sex. The way you speak to your partner and the way you look at them should show your love for them. Winking at your spouse is one way to show love. Intimacy should not only be experienced in bed. It goes beyond that. When you are sexually bonded with your spouse you become closer friends and confidants. You value each other more, and demonstrate more affection. These are some of the many ways love can be shown.

Husbands should remember that sexual intimacy also involves kissing your wife without expecting to have sex. Exercise self control. This will encourage your wife to kiss you, because she will not expect that every kiss or touch will lead to sex, on every occasion.

ROMANCE

Be affectionate, even if you are not going to have sex, be affectionate; arouse each other both emotionally and physically. A woman needs to be touched sensitivity and tenderness. It is easy a woman to tell whether you're being affectionate or mechanical. Caress each other. Touch her fingers, kiss them, and make sure you are both giving and receiving romantic gestures. Talk about how much you enjoy each other's bodies.

Before sex, take time to romance your wife. Women are like electric cookers and men are like gas cookers. When you put on a gas cooker it brings its fire straight away. Men will quickly erect and after the climax, they cool down straight way. But an electric cooker will take some time to heat up and cool down. Women are very much the same. It takes time for her to get roused, and after she reaches climax, you still need to touch her to cool down. Husbands, you need to touch your wife on all her sensitive parts, especially the clitorises and nipples, but remember to be gentle. Kissing is biblical. In Song of Solomon 1:2, the woman speaks and says she longs for him to kiss her. Another translation says, "Let him drown me with his kisses." Husband prepare your wife, right from morning. Kiss her before you go to work. Woman, you can initiate sex by touching him also. The sensitive part of a man is the top of his penis and the testicles.

Prepare yourself for each other. Wear nice fragrances and perfumes, and look attractive.

"Ointment and perfume rejoice the heart…" Proverbs 27:9. You can also read Song of Solomon 1:12, 4:1, 7.

Keep your bodies hygienic for one another, shave and mind your breath. Put the kids to bed early. Ladies wear a sexy night dress with the intention of pleasing your husband. Find many ways to enticing him; he is yours. Learn how to attract his attention. For example, you can be playful by standing where he can see you, pretending that you have dropped something. They pick it up; while bending over with your bum facing him; you'll be giving him an invitation, because men go by what they see. It's your place as a wife to seduce your man. If you don't do these things and you take your man for granted, there's a woman somewhere on the street with a mission to steal your man. You have a license girl! Go for it, don't shy away. Darling, let me repeat this, there's a prostitute on a mission looking for your man; she will do all she can to take your king. So wake up. Have sex anytime as long as your children are in bed. Anytime is the right time. No excuses ladies, just go for it! Sometimes the reason why women dodge sex is because husbands want to gratify themselves; they are not patient or truly affectionate. They just jump on their wives as if they are dogs. In the end, women start giving excuses such as "I have a headache," or "I am tired." Husbands, you will settle best results when you prepare your wife right from the morning. This includes helping her with domestic work, because she will get tired occasionally. And avoid being aggressive.

CREATIVITY

Be creative in your sex life. You can't enjoy the same meal everyday because it becomes boring and it's not healthy. The same thing can happen when having sex.

If that's what you both prefer, well, it is your choice. But it would be good if you try other styles. There's a good Christian book, *"Intended for Pleasure"* by Ed Wheat. M.D. and Gaye Wheat, it talks about these issues in more detail.

A woman of God gave a testimony in one of our marriage seminars; of how her and her husband were believing in God for a baby girl. One day the Holy Spirit gave her a word of wisdom that they should change the style of sex they normally used. She was obedient, and got pregnant with a baby girl. Why do we think God is not in our beds? In fact, He is happy to see you have sex. If you are sensitive to the Holy Spirit, He will instruct you on how to make love, and how to please your mate sexually. He is the best teacher; after all, He initiated marriage.

INITIATING SEX

One of you should initiate sex. As I said earlier on in this book, ladies tend to shy away from doing this. When a woman initiates sex, she makes her husband feel good - he feels loved. Wives, help your partner by showing him what he needs to do to make you enjoy him. Put on the lights if that's what you want. Some ladies shy away from this but, ask God to give you boldness. Make lively movements; don't be like a piece of wood. Make romantic whispers but don't be loud. You can even play some soft Christian music in the background.

Be senual and sexy with your spouse. Many women are not always in the mood when their husbands are in need. They give all sorts of excuses. Because lately women are also working; it is true that sometimes they get tired and can't meet their spouses' needs. But if you keep on denying your spouses sex, they will be tempted to commit adultery.

"Defraud ye not one the other, except it be with consent for a time, that ye may give yourselves to fasting and prayer; and come together again, that Satan tempt you not for your incontinency." 1 Corinthians 7:5

If you can't meet the need of your spouse, it has to be by mutual consent; and let that be for a specific period. Denying your spouse sex will lead your partner into temptation. For example, a man can be tempted into watching pornography because you are not being sexually affectionate on a daily basis. Some women always make excuses like, "My head is aching," and "Today in the office it was so hectic." If you do this, you quickly send a message that you don't what anything to do with him sexually. But we have the grace of God available to us. Ask God for it, so that He will strengthen you to do your duty as a wife. You can do all things through Christ who strengthens you. (Philippians 4:13). When you're genuinely tired, your man will know, because you don't give excuses all the time. Other women hide behind the excuse of fasting.

Husbands understand this; women need full sex which includes, orgasm - which is brought on by touching, kissing and tenderness. How often do you have sex? Try to come up with ideas both of you, enjoy, and make an agreement to try some new ideas out.

TIREDNESS

Keep your man satisfied. Meet his needs so that he goes out each day with his cup full. If you do this, the when there is a day that you do feel tired, when you tell him he will understand. When he is satisfied, he will not lust after ladies, even those in mini skirts; unless he is addicted to sex. If so, then he will have to open up to you and his pastors to be prayed for to receive deliverance. Or if it is the wife with the same problem, the same can be done. Appreciate his sexual needs. Men should also aim to meet their wives' sexual needs. Some ladies also have high sex drives. You aim should always by to appreciate the sexual needs of your spouse.

ORGASM

Men need to be careful to show sensitivity to their wives; and not get carried away and climax before she is satisfied. Don't be anxious for your wife to have an orgasm, rather make her enjoy it and let it come naturally. Pressing her will put her off because she will not relax. In the end, she may will give up trying. It is enjoyable if you can both reach climax at the same time. You can time it, it is interesting and sweet. Aim to climax at the same time. With whatever you do, remember your aim is to satisfy one another.

Some women take a long time to reach an orgasm. A man should not be put off by this, or give up but do whatever he can to help her enjoy intimately. Men look for sensitive areas on her body; you can ask her. During our marriage seminars, couples ask me whether it's okay to watch sexy films to spice things up. This is not biblical. First of all, these people are not Christians. As you watch them, evil spirits can be transferred to you. Secondly, you don't need to watch these films to learn. You can attend seminars, go for marital counseling or read Christian books.

As a wife, do communicate to your husband and tell him what turns you on. Don't ignore one another's requests. These are things that cause problems in marriage. And as you reach climax, don't make a lot of noise if you have children in the house, because they may hear.

Just as it doesn't take a man very long to be aroused, it doesn't take him very long to recover. He can be ready to mow the lawn, take a shower, or roll over and sleep very quickly after his orgasm. This is not the same for females. Just as it took her a longer period to get aroused it will take her a while to recover. Recovery happens as a person returns to their unerotic state.

After sex, appreciate each other. Have a bath together; clean him and let him clean you. This will depend on your culture, but do what you are comfortable with.

After all the fun you have had, this is a very good time to share. And for women, a good time to ask for something you want from your husband. It is the right time because he is relaxed. One time the Lord told me to go to the Unites States of America during Christmas time, and to me it didn't make sense. How could I leave my husband to go and visit America? But after praying, the Holy Spirit gave me wisdom and told me, "Wait until Peter is relaxed then present your request. I have already ministered to his heart." I did exactly what the Lord told me and guess what? He asked me when I wanted to go and how much it would cost. He even advised me to go with the children. He paid our tickets and we arrived in Atlanta Georgia. It's when I was there that God opened up for me a great door, that even today, I sit back and wonder how God works in miraculous ways.

What things prevent couples from enjoying sex?

1. CLEANLINESS

Keep yourself clean. As soon as you come back from work, go for a shower. You don't want to meet your mate sweaty. They will be put off. Always have a proper wash before having sex. Cleanliness is next to godliness.

The following is a true testimony. I got permission from the couple to write it. I counseled a wife who was fed up of meeting her husband intimately because he never shaved his armpits and private parts. He was always sticky and smelly. He had a bath once a week, and so every time he came close to her, she would feel like vomiting. When they were newly married, the husband was different. But it seems it was his habit not to bath. When he finally got used to his wife, he went back to his old routine. This created a problem in their sex life. God believes in clean people, look at the scripture below.

"...and you shall have an implement among your equipment, and when you sit down outside, you shall dig with it and turn and cover your refuse. For the Lord your God walks in the midst of your camp, to deliver you and give your enemies over to you; therefore your camp shall be holy, that He may see no unclean thing among you, and turn away from you."
Deuteronomy 23:13-14

Some people are not teachable. When you sit them down to advise on how to bathe they say, 'I know everything.' That's a lie, you can never know everything. Everyday we learn, "learning stops when you are dead," someone once said; and I agree, These people are not teachable; and when you're not teachable you're not reachable.

Men are advised to wash their penises. Those who are not circumcised need to open the upper skin and wash it thoroughly and then dry it, or else it can make you smell. Circumcision is beneficial as it stops some infections like Aids, as well as others.

2. IGNORANCE

Being ignorant about sex can hinder your enjoyment of it. In our African setting for example, we grew up being told that 'sex was a sin and very bad'. It was not made clear to us why. Our parents never talked about it. And so we grew up with that negative attitude. They should have told us that sex outside of marriage is a sin.

4. UNRESOLVED ISSUES

If you have misunderstandings early in the day and failed to resolve them, when the time to make love comes, you will find it hard to be affectionate. Your mate will remember how hostile you were, and you may replay things that was done that upset you. This will drive away the desire for sex. But if you learn how to praise one another, call each other in the day, and send text message saying, "I cannot wait to see you tonight, you mean a lot to me." Husband's send your wife a note at her work saying, "Hey girl I enjoy your love." If you had a misunderstanding before you went to work, keep calling each other. One of you should take the initiative. God will honor you for humbling yourself. He will give you more grace in every thing you do.

"But He gives more grace. Therefore He says: "God resists the proud, but gives grace to the humble." James 4:6

"But He gives us more and more grace (power of the Holy Spirit), to meet this evil tendency and all others fully." James 4:6 Amplified

Another reason why some men have problems in their sex life is because there are problems outside the bedroom getting in the way. They could be debts, conflicts and the like. All these can make him lose morale. If you have issues in your marriage, why not turn them to God in prayer? *"...cast all your care upon Him, for He cares for you"* (1 Peter 5:7). Don't give up. Continue praying and fasting, your breakthrough is coming. We are told that we who call upon the Lord should not keep silent, and give Him no rest till He establishes Jerusalem and makes her the praise of the earth. Isaiah 62:6:7

"Cast thy burden upon the LORD, and He shall sustain thee: He shall never suffer the righteous to be moved." Ps 55:22.

Let go of your disappointments, and fears. God is in control. You cannot carry your problems alone; but God can. Jesus told us not to allow our hearts to be troubled; but to believe in God, and also believe in Him (John 14:1). God cares about your marriage. He is the God of families. He cares about your sex life. He wants you to be happy and enjoy life to the fullest.

Never keep quiet if you have sexual problems with your partner, rather your spouse so that you can resolve the issue together. If it gets to the point where you need to seek professional advice, do not be afraid to do that. Every problem is always solvable.

5. DEMONIC ATTACKS

If you fail to forgive one another, you open yourselves up to the devil, and will therefore fail to enjoy the fulfillment that God has for you. Many couples have had this experience. A lady told me that every time she would have sex with her husband she would feel a sharp pain. She consulted a doctor, they did a thorough check but all was in vain; they found no cause. She was prayed for, and the next time she had sex, never felt the pain again. This was an attack from the devil.

A brother who couldn't function for sometime was prayed for and when he met his wife for intimacy God had healed him. This was a demonic attack because even the doctors had failed to identify the problem. Only the Lord Jesus, the greatest physician, could heal him. So, watch out. The devil came to steal, kill and destroy - therefore protect you home by submitting to God and resisting the devil, so that your marriage does not fall prey.

6. AROUSAL PROBLEMS

This can happen once in a while, especially for first time couples. Don't shy away from your spouse. Do everything you have learnt. Remember that you both went through pre-marital counseling; your partner is practicing what they learnt. If as a husband you discover that she is not a virgin, don't start asking her questions now because when you were in courtship, these are the things you should have talked about.

It can become annoying and embarrassing, for a man when he fails to have an erection. Relax or else, it will get worse. The devil can try to take advantage of this. A wife needs to be careful about what she tells her husband because how she deals with this can either completely put him off, or help him to erect. Don't say words like, "What's wrong with you? Every time we make love you don't erect," or "you don't love me," or "are you having an affair?"

The best approach to take is to hold his genital organs smoothly. You can use baby oil or Vaseline to rub on him. As you do this, speak romantic words to him; kiss his nipples, and his ears, etc. Make sure the lights are on so that you see each other. Men are stimulated visually. It will help him to erect. If all this fails, consult a doctor as soon as possible. Pray and commit this issue to God. Don't worry; God is able to heal him and help your situation.

7. DRUGS AND ALCOHOL

Drugs and alcohol can have a huge impact on sex. I once counseled a couple, and later found out that the husband was addicted to drugs and alcohol before he came to the Lord. He had even been to a rehabilitation centre. When he gave his life to Jesus, he was delivered, but the damage has been done. The Holy Spirit revealed to me that alcohol and drugs was causing their sexual problems. It is said that drugs substantially increase sexual desire but I also discovered that the opposite can occur. Ultimately, our bodies are temples of the Holy Sprit. We are not supposed to defile them by taking drugs. Drugs will ruin your body, but God is able to heal that damaged body when you repent and seek his help. You can also see the doctor to help you on this matter.

8. PER-MATURE EJACULATION

Some men fail to control their ejaculation and this can cause problems because the chances are, the wife will not be satisfied. When a man loses control, and climaxes too quickly, it devastates his ego and confidence.

A brother with this problem was advised by the doctor to relax. The doctor had discovered that he had problems at home. He was always worried, anxious and stressed. He put into practice what the doctor told him and was able to receive his healing. We had also prayed with him, and surely God performed wonders. Sometimes premature ejaculation can be caused by psychological ill-health, as well as physical problems. To remedy this, you learn to control yourself; and allow your mind to relax. Also see a medical doctor for advice.

9. DRYNESS DURING SEX IN A WOMAN

Dryness is when a woman is unable to produce enough lubricating sexual fluid during intercourse. This can be caused when a man is not able to sexually arouse his wife. Some ladies are dry because they require a great deal of sexual stimulation which cannot normally be achieved with the common sexual practices, while others have low levels of the hormone that is responsible for increased fluid secretion. You can buy lubricating tubes or Vaseline from the pharmacy to use. They can be used to lubricate the penis or vagina, which makes sexual intercourse more pleasurable. Harsh climatic conditions like high temperatures are not good for women; in fact while talking to my female doctor on this issue she told me that, "It is okay for a woman to stay without panties at home because it helps her to get some fresh air." She also said wearing tight pants can also contribute to dryness. STDs/STI's are the worst causes of dryness. If you have such a problem and you have tried all the solutions discussed and not seen any results, see your doctor.

10. PREGNANCY

Some women have complicated pregnancies at certain stages and therefore fail to have sex with their husbands. They lose the desire. Where this happens, husband need to exercise some understanding towards their wives. If you have early complications, see a doctor for advice.

11. ADULTERY IN MARRIAGE

It is so sad to hear that among us Christians and even the ministers of the gospel, there's infidelity. Wives and husbands are having extra-marital affairs. Don't try to seek fulfillment outside your marriage by giving your money and time to another person. Honour your marriage and God by remaining faithful - even through difficult times. God said, "Live happily with the woman (or man!) you love…" (Ecclesiastes 9:9). Think; when your partner gets to know about your unfaithful behaviour, you will lose their respect and trust. And trust is an extremely nard thing to rebuild once damaged. You may feel happy for a time, but my dear, what is hidden in dark will be revealed and brought into the light, eventually. Your habit will grow. Stop your lies and change. *"The lips of truth shall be established for ever: but a lying tongue is but for a moment" Proverbs 12:19.* Did you know that the acts of the righteous will bring them life? But the evil acts of the wicked will bring them punishment.

One cause of adultery is when we get so tired by the time we get into bed. We fail to be intimate with our mates. So whatever you plan to do, limit your schedule. Set your priorities right. Husband, you have to understand that there are times when your wife can't meet your need. We will look at the hindrances below. Otherwise, in order to avoid temptations, have sex regularly, enjoy each other and have fun.

Husbands can also come back home tired, stressed or sometimes frustrated after a long day. Wives, in such cases be understanding, don't rush your man, allow him to settle down. You can then share your challenges of the day, and move onto intimacy later.

If you don't meet your partner's needs, there are other women and men who are ready to seduce your partner with their words and the way they dress and conduct themself. Let's not give the devil a chance. Haven't you heard of sisters who go to visit at awkward hours, when they know the wife is not at home? How about some evil minded secretaries? As a secretary or church administrator, you were entrusted with that position, NOT to use it as an opportunity to seduce the men of God. That's why it is important, man of God, to always be with your armour bearer when counseling ladies. Be with your wife or another male minister. If possible, fix a hidden camera in the office so that the devil will not be able to damage you and your ministry. The Bible says free yourself, deliver thyself as a roe from the hand of the hunter (Proverbs 6:5). My brother, be quick to discover such spirits and inform your wife if you have fallen into sin. Your wife will put in place some corrective measures so that the mistake is not repeated. Husband, don't justify yourself because this make matters worse. Be honest with your wife; admit the wrong or else this situation can completely tear your relationship apart. When you ask your wife for forgiveness, it shows humility and God will forgive you and give you a second chance. Don't ever do it again! It is devastating, leads to psychological torture, and can be very embarrassing. Such a husband will also need to understand that it takes time for your wife to heal. If you keep on committing the same sin on the pretence that you will repent this will only put you in bondage and could result in the end of your marriage.

"YOU MUST NEVER FIND TIME FOR ANYTHING. IF YOU WANT TIME YOU MUST MAKE IT."
-BUXTON-

Don't expect your wife to trust you simply because she has forgiven you. Hear this brother, forgiveness is a decision, but trust is a process; when it's been demolished it takes time to rebuild. If you sit on a chair and it collapses beneath you, you don't hold a grudge against the chair, but when you want to sit down again you'll approach it with caution. Men and women often perceive trust differently. When a woman has been hurt, her husband may think an apology should immediately enable her to trust him again and move on. Not so Sir, you need to acknowledge what you've done! Don't just tell your wife to 'get over it.' Acknowledge her pain. Why? Because, when you make it of little importance, it hurts the more and makes her angrier. Only when you understand her, will her wounds begin to heal.

As a wife, you need to make sure that bitterness doesn't creep in! How can you do that? By refusing to stay 'broken' any longer than absolutely necessary, and by allowing God to heal your heart and restore your love.

My sister, if your man opens up to you, please don't start a fight. Appreciate the fact that he has opened up to you. And please don't attack the female concerned. Pray, and if you have a trusted elderly lady in the church, confide in her and tell her to talk to the girl.

Be careful brothers, especially pastors. A sister can come up with a false accusation and only God can help you escape such a snare or trap. And if you have already been falsely accused, the Lord will bring forth His truth and light. Wait for Him. Be strong and take heart. He will vindicate you.

"With her much fair speech she caused him to yield, with the flattering of her lips she forced him. He goeth after her straightway, as an ox goeth to the slaughter, or as a fool to the correction of the stocks;

Till a dart strike through his liver; as a bird hasteth to the snare, and knoweth not that it is for his life."
Proverbs 7:21-24

The devil is after your ministry, reputation and job, etc. Do not let your heart turn aside to the ways of a seductress her ways. The Bible says, do not stray into her paths, she will ruin your life, job, marriage, and ministry. The Bible says, her house is the road to destruction and heads to the game.

What are you looking for that is not in your wife? If she doesn't have it, put it there. If it is the hair you admired from a woman, encourage your wife to improve hers. What you sow today you will reap tomorrow. Stop running after girls, or else when your own grow; the same thing will happen to them.

If you neglected your partner and have been sexually unfaithful, you need to repent. Secondly, go to the doctors for a check-up because you may have contracted an STD. You have to be kind enough to avoid infecting your mate. Don't feel condemned over this issue but the truth will set you free.

Forgiveness

This is one of the things you need to achieve success. "Success comes to those who become success conscious." If you want to be successful in your marriage or have decided to separate; forgive. We are the salt of the world and have to work hard in our marriages so that we don't lose the flavors in it. You lose flavor in your marriage when you fail to forgive, trust your spouses, or meet his or her needs.

"Salt is good: but if the salt have lost his flavour, wherewith shall it be seasoned? It is neither fit for the land, nor yet for the dunghill; but men cast it out. He that hath ears to hear, let him hear." Luke 14:34

Ask God to give you a forgiving heart. It will not come easy, but if you let the Holy Spirit work on you, with time you will forgive and will heal. What you hate you become, but what you forgive you are released from. This means that you are released when you forgive, but when you hate, you waste time.

Why are we facing such problems? How have we opened a door to the devil to come into our homes? Why have husbands and wives failed each other? You have likely asked yourselves so many questions, but I believe we can get some answers. After counseling many couples, I now understand that there are things we do in ignorance that have caused our partners to fallprey. We shall see what these things are in our next chapter.

Pornography

Some people become adulterous because they watch porn movies and get addicted to them. It is not godly to watch pornography. Some men and women hide while they watch or read porn. They think it's a beneficial and

"THERE'S NO SIGHT ON EARTH MORE APPEALING THAN THE SIGHT OF A WOMAN MAKING DINNER FOR SOMEONE SHE LOVES"
-THOMAS WOLFE-

fulfilling experience that should be shared with their spouses. But it is filthy and dirty, it is plain sick and perverted. And is addictive. It will instill wrong ideas about making love and could make a man want to have sex at the wrong time and with anyone. Spirits will be transferred to you as you watch them.

Some husbands are never affectionate. They are after sex with no romance. Some women have this problem too. It is a spirit that follows them from their family. They are never satisfied. All they think about is sex. They even become abusive. Some husbands and wives have confessed to being addicted to watching pornographic movies. They are not affectionate, and their love making is more lust than love. They watch dirty movies before or during sex. Pornography is evil, it is a sin. It destroys your love for your spouse, marriage and self. Make your marriage an exciting place where both of you are eager to go.

I have heard stories of some women complaining about their husband's addiction to sex. They don't want to pray or even read the Bible. When they see other women, they lust after them. This is a sin because sex now becomes an idol before God. Such a man needs deliverance.

There was a woman who had a demanding husband. No matter how many times she met with him intimately, the husband was never satisfied. Whenever she tried to tell him that she was really tired, he would get so violent. He would say that it was her duty to meet his needs. Yes, it's true we are to meet our husband's sexual desires but it shouldn't go to an extreme whereby husbands start being abusive, and all they think about is sex, without considering the feelings of their wives.

Another woman told me that her husband said she had no right to say no to him, whether she was ill or not. The poor woman was made to meet her husband's selfish sexual need despite how she felt. In this type of marriage, there's no true love and intimacy, because the Bible tells us that love is kind and patient. Husbands, if your wife is truly ill, please be patient with her. If she is tired, let her rest and then encourage her later. Try to be understanding. Romans 12:10-12 says, *"Be kindly affectionate to one another with brotherly love, in honor giving preference to one another; not lagging in diligence, fervent in spirit, serving the Lord; rejoicing in hope, patient in tribulation, continuing steadfastly in prayer…"* As I said earlier, ladies don't make it as an excuse all the time by saying you are tired or you have headaches. Headaches don't just come at nights! Stop lying to your husbands. God hears your lies. What you confess is what you get.

Did you know that according to research, "a man thinks about sex every 15 minutes?" Wow! Did you read that my sister? Please read it again and may the Lord give you more grace to meet your spouse's need.

Consequences
We live in such a cruel world. Decisions are made without any thought about the consequences. This makes my heart bleed that a person will compromise their relationship with God and their family. Your family is humiliated and devastated When your immoral behaviour comes to light. You lose your integrity and sometimes your marriage. You can lose your job as well if you are in a key position, especially in the governments of the western world.

When our young people witness this, they get a poor view of marriage. There have been scenarios of men in high profile positions who choose to buy young 'call girls' or have secret mistresses and ended getting caught; yet the media pays the "call girls" big sums of money to sell their stories and become famous. What message do they send to our young girls? If we don't pray and speak to them, the devil will feed them his lies about making quick money and becoming celebrities through prostitution and harlotry

Chapter 13

ISSUES THAT HAVE CAUSED COUPLES TO FALL PREY

After waiting upon the Lord concerning this topic, the Lord led me to some issues that cause couples to fall into temptation. Sometimes we neglect some things in our relationships and before we know it, the devil is at work in our homes. But I am glad that God is faithful. He reveals to us the tactics of the devil. Be encouraged and know that God, who started the good work in your home, will bring it to completion.

How have we opened a door to the devil to come into our sexual relationship? Have we failed each other? There are many unanswered questions but, I believe, we can find the answers. After going through counseling sessions with couples, I discovered some of the issues. We will look at each one in turn.

DENYING YOUR MATE SEX

You must understand that denying your spouse sex is a sin; you lead them into temptation. Once you are married your body is no longer just your own.

"Let the husband render unto the wife due benevolence: and likewise also the wife unto the husband. The wife has not power over her own body, but the husband: and likewise also the husband has not power of his own body, but the wife. Defraud all of you not one the other, except it be with consent for a time, that all of you may give yourselves to fasting and prayer; and come together again, that Satan tempt you not for your incontinency 1 Corinthians 7:3-5.

Woman your husband has a need and it's your responsibility to meet it. Medical research says a man can think about sex every 15 minutes. It is a command to meet your partner's sexual needs. One day God opened my eyes to understand that I was sinning by denying my husband sex. There are times I would feel so tired because of my schedule, by the time I got in bed I would be worn out. Instead of telling my husband the truth, I would feign illness until the Holy Spirit rebuked me. First, for not speaking the truth that I was tired, secondly, for not being understanding that my husband was in need. He told me the day I got married I relinquished my right to withhold my body from my husband. At times I would withhold or deny physical affection, if we engaged in an argument. But I had change, as God was not pleased.

We are instructed to settle our arguments before we go to bed so that we can enjoy our spouses, as God intended. Sometimes it can be hard but you can ask God to give you the grace to forgive, so that you can go ahead and have fun with your mate. Someone out there wishes they were in your shoes. They wish they were married to your man. Sometimes you may feel like you don't want to have sex, but in the process of doing it you will end up enjoying yourself.

FAILING TO BE CREATIVE

Make your sex creative. Sex in marriage is an opportunity for genuine love making. Try different styles, and new movements that will excite your spouse. It is important that you fully satisfy your mate, this way you never have to worry about them straying or being sexually frustrated. Avoid being boring; it can lead your partner into temptation. You might have come into marriage after you had been involved in other relationships, and because of that, the devil can attack your mind and cause you to compare your partner to others. This is why it's important as Christians for us to keep ourselves holy unto the Lord, and to wait for our future partners; or else the devil can use impurity to torment us. It is wrong to compare your mate to another. You may not mention it, but it can be in your mind as you are with your partner; and you might be thinking about your former boyfriend or girlfriend. This is not good. There are cases where especially husbands have come to our counseling sessions and admitted that for them to reach a sexual climax, they had to first think about their former girlfriends because their wives were not sexually exciting or creative. If you find yourself struggling in this area, you need to repent, bring into captivity your thoughts, to the obedience of Christ.

Never make sex a mundane routine. If you do you risk boring your mate. Failing to understand these issues can cause problems in our marriages and, in the end,has the potential to cause separation and divorce.

Thank God for His grace, His grace is what will help you through the rough times in your marriage. Paul acknowledged this when he spoke of his 'thorn in the flesh' (2 Corinthians 12:7). Has your partner messed around? This can be painful, so you need to ask God for this grace to heal and help you. 'My grace (my sustaining care) is sufficient for thee…' (2 Corinthians 12:9).

Grace is what enables you to love an abusive mate, keep waiting for the stubborn teenager to come back, endure prolonged illness, live with little yet give much, overcome disappointments, and forgive repeated offences. Grace takes you beyond your natural ability by forcing you to rely on God's strength alone.

DECEPTIVE FRIENDS

Be careful what friends you bring near your spouse. Many people are different from what they appear. The world is full of phony, deceptive people who are out to get your partner.

"I CAN LIVE FOR TWO MONTHS ON A GOOD COMPLIMENT."
-MARK TWAIN-

Be careful not to leave your friends alone with your husband to often; not even your own sisters - the same principle applies to them also. Some of us go overboard and we leave our spouses with anyone. That's not wise. Don't give the devil a chance. Be wise. I am not saying friends or your siblings are bad. But it is better to be safe than sorry. You need friends around you who encourage you through intercession and through laughter. Be careful not to share your marital problems with just any friends. But of course, if you are close enough to a married friend who you can trust, then pour your heart out; but ensure that whatever you share is clearly understood, and is not misinterpreted. Never gossip about your spouse; it is dangerous.

Your husband must be the first friend you share with;

although you also need female friends because there are some things that men don't understand about women. For example, the state you go through when you have just had a baby or the labour pains you endure. Men don't think like women. As a woman you need a female friend to share with, but select someone your husband trusts. Avoid turning to a friend on a consistent basis, before turning to God when you experience marital problems. God is a jealous God, and He should be the first to be approached concerning your worries.

Having godly friends is a great benefit. You will need them. Women need their girl friends and men need their male friends. Ultimately, you need to learn how to balance things by knowing where to draw a line, in your friendships. This includes when to visit, and for how long. We have all heard stories of friends that were trusted but ended up messing up their friends' marriages. But if you find godly friends they will be a great asset because when you need them they will stand with you through thick and thin. Good friends will help you reach your destiny. Protect and love them. There's a saying, "In the good times our friends know us, in the bad times, and we know our friends."

If you don't have friends, you tend to focus on your own desires, problems and needs. You can become self-focussed, which is selfishness. And God would rather have you help your friends when they have problems. Help meet their needs; rather than preoccupying yourself with your own world. Spend some time cultivating friendships. A true friend will help you see your good qualities and your weaknesses. God can use your friend to minister to you. It has happened to me so many times. I have a friend who corrects me and helps me to stay on track and in the right direction.

As much as you have friends, always remember to draw a line; listen to your conscience. If you become uncomfortable or start feeling a warning about a friend who is close to your partner, please watch out; in most cases, God is warning you.

LACK OF TIME TOGETHER

As pastor, I have counseled many couples and the majority of them are in full time work. I have noticed that people in London work so hard and if we are not careful marriages will be wounded or even lost. I am not against working but we need to use wisdom. In some families the husband works in the day and the wife works at night from the beginning of the year to the end. In this day and age work schedules often tend to be different than the typical nine-to-five jobs of previous generations. Couples therefore rarely meet.

And even if they meet they are so tired they don't have time for each other. Often what results is divorce. You need to learn how to balance and prioritise. Why don't both of you sit down and come up with a plan; for example, to believe God for another job. Nothing is impossible with God. He is able to give you a better job that allows you more enough time to spend with your spouse. Don't give your whole heart and soul to work, leaving precious little room for youself and the family. Some husbands and wives have become workaholics. Cut back on work and invest more time and energy into your marriage and personal life. Don't allow work to pre-occupy your wide life. Even if you've had a very busy day - relax!

OVER DELEGATING

This issue is more relevant to women. When you are married avoid leaving all the household chores to your maid and children. If you have a maid, supervise and assit her. Make sure that dinner is well prepared and that tasks around the house are being done properly.

When your husband arrives home after a long day, take time to welcome him back. Men, as a husband if you arrive home first before your wife, welcome her back. You have nothing to lose! If for any reason a man is out of work, he should make it his duty to assist with work in the home. If as a man you feel undermined by the idea of helping out with work around the house; consider 'what would Jesus do?'

Also, exercise wisdom by not allowing a maid to become too close to your husband. Not all maids are to be trusted alone with your husband. But even if the maid has no bad intentions, if you leave her to do every thing, you run the risk of leading them into temptation. Be well aware of these issues and guard your marriage accordingly. Your husband, is human and so are you. If you are already suspicious that any inappropriate behaviour is going on between your maid and your husband, tell her to leave immediately. Speak to your husband about it and if he is not willing to change, then present the issue to your pastors. You may also want to seek professional Christian counseling.

If you are not happy to have a female maid around the house, the natural response might be to employ a male helper. However, other issues may arise. I would suggest you do not employ a male to work for you if you have little girls. I have heard of many cases where families have had problems, where their little girls where raped, or impregnated.

Mothers I encourage you to tell your daughters about

the temptations they can face wherever they go. Also fathers need to be strong and not give the devil a chance to lead them into temptation. I have heard of incidents where a step father had an affair with his step daughter. I thank God for my mum, who taught us about such things when we were young. She used to tell us that if you go to visit your sister always stay with her. If her husband calls you in the bedroom don't go. So we grew up knowing that getting too close to a man was not a very good idea. Young girls should be made away of the dangers they face, because they can be vulnerable.

Whether you are tired or not, aim to do as many things for your husbands as you can. Your maid should not be doing more for your husband than you do. Things such as setting the bath, should always be the duty of a wife. You have to be wise, don't allow your maid to be too involved with your husband, if she has a bad agenda, you will give her the opportunity to tempt Him, without you even being aware. Be careful. This has happened to a lot of women, especially career women that come home very tired. The devil is like a roaring lion, ever looking for someone to devour. However tired you may be, stay with your man. If you feel too weary to respond to your husband's call, then call out to the Lord and request that His Spirit to refresh you, that you may enjoy sex with him. When your mind is not working due to stress overload, call out to the Lord; ask for help. Make it your goal to always have some emotional and physical energy; so that your sexual desire will not be a problem.

Men should also communicate if they feel that their wives are delegating many tasks. Be honest with your wives and let them know if you are heading into temptation. The desire for sin is more often birthed in us as a result of what we see. If you see that your maid is dressed inappropriately, bring your observations to the attention of your wife. What your eyes see affects your heart. Proverbs 4:23 advises, *"Guard your heart, for out of it flow issues of life."*

Your eyes are a window into your soul. And Satan makes every effort to expose your eyes to ungodly images in an attempt to pollute and pervert your heart.

Make a covenant with your eyes not to look on that which you are in danger of lusting after. According to the Merriam-Webster dictionary, a covenant is a written agreement or promise usually under seal between two or more parties especially for the performance of some action. It is a formal, solemn, and binding agreement. See Proverbs 23:31-33, and Mathew 5:28.

Make no room or space for any woman other than your wife. Women will only come to a man who shows interest in them. When you give them space, they discover your weaknesses. If they find you are weak or unprotective of your relationship they are likely to turn you into their business but if they know you are strict and happily married, there is no way they will persist.

FAITHFULNESS

The Bible is uncompromising in its demand for sexual faithfulness. You must be committed to giving yourself to your spouse only. Close your eyes to other men and women no woman; wants to share her husband. Adultery is strictly forbidden in the Bible. The seventh commandment given on Sinai was, "You shall not commit adultery" (Exodus 20:14). Jesus mentioned this commandment in His conversation with the rich young ruler (Matthew 19:18). And Paul named adultery first in his list of the sins of the flesh (Galatian 5:19).

COMPARIING YOUR SPOUSE

Your spouse is your spouse. No two people are the same. Every person is unique. Be satisfied with whom God has given you. Comparing your spouse with another person, can be deeply hurtful and demoralising to the one you love. What your spouse doesn't know today they will know tomorrow. Comparison with any other person will surely demoralise your partner.

BE PATIENT

Women, you don't want to get into the same mistake Sarah got into Genesis 16:3 *"Then Sarai, Abram's wife, took Hagar her maid, the Egyptian, and gave her to her husband Abram to be his wife, after Abram had dwelt ten years in the land of Canaan."* You may not give your husband a maid directly but you might do it differently. For example if your husband is delayed returning home from work, you leave your maid to open the gate for him, she wears a see through night dress, runs the bath tab, prepares your husbands dinner while wearing a prophesying dress, rolling her eyes; and what would you expect next?

On Sarah's instruction Abraham slept with Hagar, and when Hagar saw she had conceived, her mistress became despised in her eyes. Watch out if you sense your maid behaving strangely, as it could indicate that something wrong is going on. Hagar began insulting her mistress, and boasting. She acted as though she was a better woman, more favoured by heaven; and also believed that she would be better loved by Abraham. So she stopped submitting to Sarah. I bet Sarah wished she had waited on the Lord.

Sarah negatively influenced Abraham to take Hagar her maid. But she was wrong to try to provide a solution, to a problem that God had already promised to resolve in her favour. Saran and Abram didn't wait for God's timing. Even today there are many sisters who want to get married they get tired of waiting and because all their friends are getting married, they also decide to get married, and end up marrying a VMW instead of a BMW. Never make a permanent decision on a temporally situation.

Be patient knowing that, God's timing is the best. Wait for your God-ordained man; he is coming. Seek God's counsel in everything! Whom to marry, your job, changing your home, moving country, etc. Destinies are connected to places.
If you are a maid, friend or sibling, and have found yourself having an inappropriate relationship, now is your time to repent. You need to get out of that relationship. Wicked people will never prosper. When you come against a covenant you are fighting against God.

God is a God of a second chance, repent and you will receive forgiveness. You might have failed, but you can make a choice to repent, move on, and do better.

CLEANLINESS

Always have a proper wash before meeting your partner, cleanliness is next to godliness. I have already spoken on this issue.

COMPARING YOUR PARTNER TO ANOTHER

One of the biggest mistakes we do is comparing our partners with others, God is not going to make your spouses be like any one else, He wants them to be who He created them to be, and He will not help you be anyone but you. 2 Corinthians 10:12, reminds us that we are not called to compete with others, but to love and help each other. You are unique, and so is your spouse. Stop looking at other people and admiring them and comparing them, with your spouse. If you happen to see something good about someone's partner that you like, say for example; your friend's husband is wearing a double chafflike shirt; go and buy one for your man. Men if you see a lady with a good bag, or shoes you like, shop for something similar and buy it for her. If you like the way your friend's wife cooks, learn the recipe and introduce it to your wife. Be tactful, a good way to mention it might be, "I tried this food at Mr. & Mrs. B's place can we try cooking it?

My sister, if your husband makes a suggestion like this don't be offended; have a teachable spirit; unteachable people never progress very far because, they will not learn from others. When you are teachable, then you can be corrected. If you are teachable you are reachable. Learn to celebrate your partners uniqueness. We are all made differently, for a reason.

Chapter 14

GRACE TO RESOLVE CONFLICTS

It is hard to live with someone without having disagreements. There is no perfect marriage. It takes the grace of God to live with someone. Child of God, there's enough grace for you to resolve conflicts in your marriage. God's grace is sufficient for you. Remember His power is made perfect in your weakness. Rise above your shortcomings, and don't allow the enemy to take advantage of you. It is possible to live in peace as long as you are willing to pursue peace. *"Pursue peace with all people..." Hebrews 12:14.* Develop, as far as you possibly can, good understanding, in relation to your spouse and everybody else. Follow understanding; trace it through all windy circumstances; and have it with all men. Be patient with each other as, no one is perfect in this life. Love may be blind, but marriage is a real eye opener! The truth is, there are times in every marriage when you just have to grit your teeth and bare some things. Pray for grace, and remember your commitment before God.

"My grace is sufficient for you, for my power is made perfect in weakness." 2 Corinthians 12:7-9

DISAGREE TO AGREE

As partners of a relationship, you will from time to time have different opinions about things, but this should not cause problems between you. Learn to resolve conflicts tactfully. You need to be happy in your home because joy is a commodity that everybody needs. It is important and crucial in life. Two people from different backgrounds are bound to have some misunderstandings at some point in time. This is just a part of the adjustment process in marriage; two people must adjust themselves until perfect harmony is birthed. Aviod making disagreements develop into a long drawn-out quarrel. The Bible says that conflicts should be settled on the same day they arise. *"...Do not let the sun go down on your anger." Ephesians 4:26*

At the onset of any quarrel, remember what we are told in the word of God to live a life worthy of the calling to which we have been called, with lowliness and meekness, with patience, forbearing one another in love, eager to maintain the unity of the Spirit in the bond of peace. When you marry somebody, you marry everything they are and everything they've been. You inherit their strengths, their fears and their weaknesses. It's impossible to choose the parts you want and leave the ones you don't. It's a package deal.

Conflict in marriage isn't nearly as important as how you handle it. I once heard a man of God say on TBN TV station, *"Most marital conflicts don't ever get resolved. There are always issues around in-laws, children, money etc. What's crucial is keeping things positive, accept the other person's perspective, have an appropriate discussion without getting critical or blaming. Your attitude plays out over the long haul. Couples that retain mutual respect and understanding stay together."* Some people can't stand being pressurised, and therefore respond badly to conflict. If your spouse is unresponsive on an issue, discuss it with a trusted friend; then give your spouse the condensed, less emotional version. Please don't put on the armor of fight, instead, with every confrontation but put on the armor of God; and remember to pursue peace, for the sake of a happy home.

The devil has made marriage one of his prime targets. He loves to promote division and strife between couples. God's Word says, *'...Satan will not outsmart us. For we are very familiar with his evil schemes' 2 Corinthians 2:1.* God's plan for your relationship is strength and harmony, not strife and confusion. He wants to help you build a strong, loving union that glorifies Him. To do that successfully, you must resolve to make Him Lord in every area of the relationship!

I thank God for all the problems we have gone through in our marriage, all these years. I have seen God change us. Change comes in the process of trials. God has used the many trials in our marriage to transform us into His nature. Change comes from wilderness experiences, problems, tornados and so on. It is a process of transition from one level to another. When people see us today, they admire our marriage but, we have seen many challenges, one after another, yet, God has seen us through. The same God will also see you through. May the Lord give you peace that transcends all understanding as you pass through tornadoes in your marriage. I encourage you to get my book called, "In my darkest hour." In it, I talk about trials and how God delivers us and gives us victory. I believe it will help you to find rest for your souls; and be happy in a successful marriage.

There are many times when I wanted to throw in the towel and call it quits. But I'm so glad I didn't. Living with your partner for a long time is something to treasure. I have not achieved this in my life, without learning a lot, forgiving a lot and giving a lot. My husband and I have gone through storms and trials, but blessed be the name of Lord. His Holy Spirit has taught us to forgive one another and to resolve our differences. We have always called on God's grace when we have had challenges. So I encourage you do not give up! Keep going! Ask God for more grace in your marriage, and more wisdom to do what is right. What you have to remember is that anyone can and will make mistakes. Learn how to overlook small and petty arguments. Yield to the Holy Spirit. Don't be rigid! Humble yourself and let go of your anger. Be kind to each other. Give room to your spouse to make mistakes; after all, no one is perfect! Learn to be quite and of a good heart.

I have seen God's grace working in our marriage, a day never goes by, before I cry out to God for more grace in my marriage, and for my children. God has always proved faithful. After all, the disagreements, frustrations and tears, I am thankful that we pressed on. By His grace, we have not given up and we are not going to give up. To God be the glory.

In the early years of our marriage, when we had outstanding issues, and when our marriage was failing, we would approach our good and godly friends who would always be willing to stand with us in prayer. I thank God for their love, wisdom, encouragement and care. When you reach a stalemate, get input from a trusted friend or counselor, before it becomes a crisis.

Marriage is not a bed of roses. There will be problems. You will disagree but disagreements are healthy, as long as you can get to the other side, and grow from it. People who do not get along with others are only interested in themselves; they will disagree with what everyone else knows is right (Proverbs 18:1).

Conflict is a fact of life in today's marriages. Even the best of friends face conflicts, but that doesn't have to mean the end of the relationship. When conflict is not dealt with properly, it can create strained relationships, and grow to eat away the time, energy and productivity of even the best of friends.

Dealing with conflicts directly may be uncomfortable at times, and lead to some disappointment, but it cuts down the mind-reading and the resentment that can occur when problems are not tackled head on. Attempting to wait until you get a long break like Christmas season, to resolve your issues, might result in separation. Work on your issues right now or else they will catch up with you. You might take a while to tackle them head on but make sure you still keep focused on resolving any conflict. You need to be a problem solver not a problem evader. We are taught from childhood to avoid conflict, and often waver between the pain of dealing with unresolved problems and the guilt over not dealing with them. But I do believe in sitting down and resolving them. Get someone you trust to help you. If you don't allow someone to help you stop these conflicts and arguments, your marriage will face inevitable torment.

My husband is a very good problem solver. He has learnt to deal with conflicts effectively. As soon as I start disagreeing with him, he knows how to calm me down. Learn to deal with issues, and not personalities. It is all too easy to abuse your spouse instead of dealing with the real issues. It's okay to be assertive but you must affirm the rights your spouse to have different ideas, values and priorities. When you take disagreements personally and attack back, you invite escalation, and cause conflicts to become a bigger problem than they needed to. Keep the focus on mutual problem solving, and avoid name calling. And know when to admit that you are wrong.

What you have to understand is that the devil hates Christian marriages. He will fight tooth and nail to see that you don't live a happy life and that you don't live in peace together. Your living together is a big threat to the devil. *"One can chase a thousand, and two can put ten thousand to flight"* (Deuteronomy 32:30). Living in harmony with your spouse is a big loss to the devil. Remember *"We don't wrestle against flesh and blood but against principalities and wicked spiritual forces"* Ephesians 6:12. Once you know this you can turn your guns away from each other and point them at the devil. It is important to always remind ourselves of this above scripture, or else we can start fighting each other, which only results in our own defeat.

Even Jesus talked about the danger of being divided.

"And he called them unto Him, and said unto them in parables, How can Satan cast out Satan? And if a kingdom be divided against itself, that kingdom cannot stand. And if a house be divided against itself, that house cannot stand. And if Satan rise up against himself, and be divided, he cannot stand, but hath an end. Mark 3:23-27

A house where its members are divided, cannot; its open to destructive evil powers. We find our strength in working together in unity. There will always be times when you need a friend to lean on. The Bible says, *'If one…falls, the other can reach out and help' Ecclesiastes 4:10*. In a good marriage when one partner is weary in battle, the other can take over for a while. There's strength in unity. Remember, *"A person …alone can be…defeated, but two can stand back to back and conquer" Ecclesiastes 4:12.* Two people in a strong relationship can accomplish more than twice as much as they could do individually (Ecclesiastes 4:9). Every marriage has its conflicts, however, you must remember to agree to disagree, and not take conflicts personally. "People who live together will inevitably have quarrels." When you start a quarrel, think of it like breaching a dam, and therefore stop it before it goes any further. Fools love to pick fights, but it's a mark of good character to avert quarrels (Proverbs

20:3). Let go of all the arguments and let God's peace reign in you. Triggering an argument is like turning on a tap. It is better to leave it closed. Get rid of strife, it is a spirit that will transfer to your children if you let it get out of control. Quarrelling is a sin, and anyone who quarrels, loves sin. One of the causes of quarelling is often, boasting and pride (Proverbs 17:19). Boasting is not godly; it comes from pride, and God resists the proud. Pride is evil and it will destroy your marriage if you don't learn to humble yourself. Ask God to deliver you. Quarrelling brings frustration and will steal you joy and will make your family miserable. A cheerful heart is good medicine but a crushed spirit dries up the bones (Proverbs 17:22).

If your soul is weary with sorrow because of quarrels, you will need to be strengthened in God's word (Psalms 110:28). Not only does discord cause a lot of problems in a home, it also affects the ministry where the husband and wife are involved. Either party may be tempted to fight for power, and bring their striving into church.

"Time spent quarrelling is time stolen from romance," says Pastor Robert Kayanja.

When you have a dispute, don't take it to court unless it is an extreme circumstance, such as your spouse threatening to kill you. In such a situation, do not suffer in silence. Don't put your life on the line. In the case of conflicts that are not of a life threatening nature; see your pastor, or a professional Christian counselor. You should also run to God, and present your marital issues to Him, because His name is a strong tower; and when the righteous run to it, they are safe (Proverbs 18:10). Your marriage will be safe when you take it to Him in prayer, consistently. Tend to your marriage as you would tend a fig tree; which when you look after it, you eat its fruit (Proverbs 27:18). When you take care of your marriage, you will get the fruit of peace, joy, love, and new romance. As you take care of your marriage both of you and your spouse will be honored by God and those who watch you and of course God (Proverbs 27:18).

Marriage is like a garden in which grass will always grow. Your duty is to keep tending to it. When outsiders see its beauty, they will be seeing the beauty of the Lord our God. He has promised to establish the work of our hands, according to (Psalms 90:17). We will be incredibly respected and admired because of the way we handle our marriages. People will see the pleasantness and sweetness of our homes. And our marriages will be a delight to the Lord, to our well wishers, and to other observes. There are some who will hate to see your marriage blossom. They prefer to see you crying, and living in regret, and divorced. God will not allow it!

Whenever we see an admirable marriage, we ought to remember that someone worked hard to get it to where it is. Marriage is hard work; it is not for lazy people. There's a reward for working hard at your marriage. You can't always avoid getting hurt by your relationship, but God can give you the grace to re-evaluate experiences and cause you to realise that your spouse is not your enemy. Work hard on your marriage by loving and forgiving each other; and showing appreciation, and doing other things that help to build your relationship. God will reward you here on earth and in heaven. Since marriage can be hard work, it means that problems will always come, but that you need to keep on working on it. You'll need to inject some love, appreciation, forgiveness and good conflict resolution practices.

Every marriage has its issues, so never give up. We are supposed to dominate situations. Circumstances must bow to the authority of God within us. God will use the fire from situations to purify us. Go through the process in order to acquire what God wants you to do. Do not allow fear to take over you. Have the same spirit like the Hebrew boys who stood steadfast in the midst of a fiery furnace. They stood firm and so should you. Travail in prayer until you see change (Isaiah 66:8). Cry out to God, and He will respond. You might not have a clue how to solve the problem in your marriage. But God is not a liar. And without prayer, you cannot achieve much. You need to pray for yourself and not just your partner. In times of challenge look up to God, the author and finisher of our faith. By His Grace you can endure painful situations. When you receive a revelation, from there you will have a revolution. Challenges come to rob us of what God has done and is doing; but remember where God has brought you from. He has inscribed you on the palms of His hands, and He has promised to deliver the righteous from every situation.

Sometimes we create our own fire, for example, marrying someone because of his or her status. But God is good. As long as we are willing to change, He will work the situation out for our own good. All things work out for the good of those who love God. Sometimes someone has to hurt you so that you can be provoked to do what you have to do. Ugandans have a saying that: 'One who chases you also shows you the escape route.' When the devil provokes you, he is helping, by motivating you to take the action steps that will ultimately improve our lives.

WATCH YOUR WORDS

When you are talking to your spouse avoid jumping to conclusions. Don't preach, lecture or teach. Give good suggestions and wise advice but only when solicited.

Avoid accusation and criticism. Let's not just delight in airing our own opinions lest we look like fools who don't have pleasure in understanding others (Proverbs 18:2). Even in the middle of a hot argument, choose your words wisely. A gentle answer turns away anger, but a harsh response stirs it up (Proverbs 15:1). Try not to fire back when you're upset. Be slow to anger.

God doesn't deny us the right to our emotions, however He does hold us accountable for the way we handle them. Paul said, "Don't sin by letting anger gain control over you"...anger gives a mighty foothold to the devil." Satan would like nothing better than to gain an entry point into your home, and then turn it into hell. And every time you fly into a rage, you lose ground to him. Hot words don't result in cool judgment. Solomon said, *"...people with quick tempers show their foolishness" Proverbs 14:29.* The way to manage your anger is by finding ways to express it, so it doesn't end up in an explosion. It is okay to share your feelings, but you must do so wisely. Listen darling, the issue is not about who's right or wrong, or who can yell the loudest. It is about finding the answer that is best for everyone. Nobody can be everything you want them to be, all the time. It's impossible to have a long-term, loving relationship without learning to accept human weakness. So instead of dwelling on one another's shortcomings, focus on your collective strength as a family. Clinical Psychologist, Dr Paul

Pearsall says, 'Most of us would give our lives for a family member. Yet too often we live our daily life as if we take our families for granted.' Learn to control your temper; your family is worth it. After all, who else loves you regardless of what you do? And where else can you find the comfort that comes from such a support system?

'Do not let any unwholesome talk come out of your mouths, but only what is helpful.' Ephesians 4:29

Solomon said: *"Reckless words pierce like a sword...the tongue of the wise brings healing." Proverbs 12:18*

Marriage is a special relationship created by God. You're 'no longer two, but one' (Matthew 19:6), so when conflicts arise, attack the problem, not your spouse. And stay calm; that way, your partner is more likely to take you seriously. Choose the best time to address the issues; not when you're both tired and the kids are hungry. And do remember that even if you're upset it's important to consider your spouse's viewpoint. Men and women see things differently, and as such, there'll be times when you'll have to compromise. Do not let any unwholesome talk come out of your mouths at these sensitive times. Encourage one another; forgiving one another and praying for each other. Why not spur one another on toward love and good deeds? (Hebrews 10:24) Carry each other's burden, the way Jesus did for us.

Always watch what you say especially when you are annoyed. When you shout and speak angry words at your spouse it may make them withdraw, shrivel up or shut down, especially if they're already insecure. And be careful with your tone because the devil can use even the subtlest of things to upset someone. On the other hand, gracious words will help your spouse to open up. Harsh words, mood swings and attitudes will cause your spouse to keep away from you. Healthy words will promote your the longevity of relationship and revive your romance. So select what you say wisely.

"Let your speech be always with grace, seasoned with salt, that ye may know how ye ought to answer every man." Colossians 4:6

What you speak today will determine your future and will either encourage or discourage your partner. Remember, let no corrupt communication proceed out of your mouth, but that which is good for the use of edification, that it may minister grace to the hearers (Ephesians 4:29). Solomon says, *"There is that speaketh like the piercings of a sword: but the tongue of the wise is health." Proverbs 12:18*

The more you increase in knowledge and

understanding, the greater your tendency will be to spare your words. And a man of understanding is of a calm spirit (Proverbs 17:27). Remain calm, even when you have been offended. Allow your emotions to subside before you respond to any situation that bothers you. Ask the Holy Spirit to guide you as you speak. Allow Him to give you the words to say. The Bible says that even a fool is thought wise if he keeps silent, and discerning if he holds his tongue (Proverbs 17:28).

Try to be tactful when you and your partner is in a public place. If your husband or wife makes a mistake wait until you arrive home to correct them. Words are the most powerful thing in the universe, and they have the ability to hold you in bondage. When God was creating the world, He simply spoke and the world came into existence. And so man was created in the image of God; therefore we too have the same creative ability.

"In the multitude of words there wanteth not sin: but he that refraineth his lips is wise." Proverbs 10:19

You can sit around wishing that your spouse would change but do you know that they could also be wishing that you change. As much as they frustrate you, you also frustrate them. But we are told in the scriptures to live in harmony with one another in order to have good relationships, according to Romans 12:16. How do you achieve harmony? By getting rid of pride and strife and being willing to live and work well with your spouse and others. You can adjust yourself with the help of the Holy Spirit; and then your partner will also change. Paul adjusted himself and became a servant to all in order that he might win the more. To the Jews, he became as a Jew, that he might win Jews; to those who were under the law, as under the law, that he might win those who were under the law; to the weak he became weak; that he might win them. He became all things to all men, that he might by all means save some (1 Corinthians 9:19-22).

I came to know the Lord Jesus before my husband did and to win him over, the Lord revealed to me that I had to adjust on so many things, such as cutting down on what I was doing in church, so that I could spend quality time sometime with him. I was a volunteer in so many departments, some of which, God had not called me to participate. With wisdom, I left some departments and I concentrated on those that I felt God had called me to. In the end it worked for me, and for my husband who initially had started complaining about my being fully involved in the church all the time without leaving any time for family. My over-involvement in church had brought disagreements in our home but I am glad that I listened to the Holy Spirit's advice. We should always aim to be balanced because getting off balance will open us up to demonic attacks (1 Peter 5:8). If you ask the Holy Spirit to help you balance your life, he will assist you. You need to adopt and adjust yourself to your spouse. If your partner is a non–believer, you need to adjust in a way that encourages them to come to the Lord. I don't mean that you should compromise, but you do need to ask God for wisdom. He will show you areas in your life that cause disagreements and that might discourage your spouse from coming to the Lord. Things like talking negative stuff about your church, and preaching to them all the time, might not be that helpful.

Some wives are like a knife. Whatever comes out of their mouth is destructive; they are like Job's wife, the destructive nature in her manifested when she told her husband to curse God and die. Your mouth can be a blessing or a knife. Some wives have terribly toxic tongues. When your husband is talking, you're also talking. Be wise and let him talk. It is better if you wait for him to finish. Then you can wisely explain what you wanted to tell him (Proverbs 14:1). Your words can be a source of wisdom, deep as the ocean, fresh as a flowing stream (Proverbs 18:5). Many things causing couples to divorce can be avoided.

Don't envy happy couples because what you are seeing are the days of their triumph. At one point they too had their own battles to fight. They might even have them now, but they chose to be happy. Put all your effort into building your marriage, do all it takes; pray, spend time with each other and be balanced. Napoleon Hill said, "Barnes succeeded because he chose a definite goal, and placed all his energy, all his will power and all his effort into achieving that goal." To have a successful marriage there's so much you have to put into it, and the grace of God is available for you to help you.

We all have our ups and downs but on the whole you can have a happy life and you can have a lovely family. You have to work at your marriage, and think of one another as someone who is not perfect but who is trying their best. It is the grace of God that helps us improve our lives.

In the world today we are bombarded with stories of natural disasters, war, terrorism, and hurricanes; all bad news, so why not make your home a happy one? Make each other happy,

SHARE FUN AND LAUGHTER

I read an article in an English daily that said "Women do many things for their partners but making them laugh is not one of them. Their jokes hit the mark only

39% of the time, compared with 71% of those told by men. Almost half the men questioned thought they were good at telling jokes but only quarter of the women said they were funny, a survey for ocean village cruises found." This raised a question in me; if most of us don't laugh and are not funny, could it be that we are either grumpy, quarreling or nagging the men instead? This is a challenge we need to work on. Be happy, learn to crack jokes with your spouses and children. Remember a merry heart does good, like medicine, but a crushed spirit dries up the bones (Proverbs 17:22). Keep humour alive. God says, "A cheerful heart brings a smile…a sad heart makes it hard to get through the day" Proverbs 15:13. When you're experiencing many woes, family problems, illness or plain old exhaustion, humor eases the tension and restores perspective.

Teach yourself to be happy, no matter what. Do not allow the devil to steal your joy, David also prayed and said, restore to me the joy of my salvation. When some men come home, they bring all their frustrations to their wives. Some rarely laugh or joke with their wives, forgetting that it is to a man's honor to avoid strife. But if we are quick to quarrel, the Bible calls us fools (Proverbs 20:19).

Let your heart be at peace; it gives life to your body (Proverbs 14:30). In the midst of all the challenges of life today, we need God's peace to reign in our hearts and homes. In the world today, there's a lot of unhappiness. People are filled will hatred, bitterness, anger, fear, resentment and the like. As we associate with them, let us discourage them not to take their frustrations home at the end of the day.

TEMPER

A quick-tempered man acts foolishly (Proverbs 14:17). Haven't you heard of people who get so worked up, they end up killing their children unintentionally? They can't control their temper and end up in prison. How about those who decide to take their own lives because of their hot and uncontrollable temper? When they fail to come to agreement with their partners, for example concerning finances, the next thing you hear is they have committed suicide. This usually is caused by a person being anxious that before you know it, they get so depressed that they end up taking their own life. Worry, according to the Bible, weighs a person down; but an encouraging word cheers a person up (Proverbs 12:25).

If you don't pray against anger, a bad temper and wrath, you end up in destruction. The Bible warns us to be careful! Watch out for attacks from the devil, your great enemy. He prowls around like a roaring lion, looking for some victim to devour. Take a firm stand against him, and be strong in your faith. Remember that your Christian brothers and sisters all over the world are going through the same kind of suffering you are (1 Peter 5:8).

When you see your partner getting out of control, it's better to start keeping quiet, pray in your heart for God's peace to intervene quickly. Secondly, walk away until after everything calms down. Then you can raise the matter when the environment is more conducive. Ask God to give you wisdom and the right words to use. The heart of the wise teaches his mouth and adds learning to his lips (Proverbs 16:23). A good word makes a man's heart glad(Proverbs 12:25). This means God's wisdom (His word) will teach your heart, and His word and promises will influence your speech to transmit that learning to your lips. The word of God in you will teach or control your speech and conduct.

We need to study God's word and meditate on it because we need it in times like these. The Holy Spirit will remind us, and bring out of our banks (hearts) what we have stored to bail us out of this critical condition. Then we shall be able to use pleasant, sweet words (Proverbs 16:24) and they will promote our relationships, or release of divine grace in our daily living. This will lead both of you to a victorious life, through a consistent acknowledgment of the power and might of God, with both mouth and manner.

HONOR GOD WITH YOUR WORDS

King David prayed and asked God to help him make the words of his mouth and the meditation of his heart acceptable in His sight. Psalms 19:14. Our words and thoughts should align with God's word and will. This text literally means, "let what I speak and what my heart murmurs to itself be a delight to you Lord." Clearly, the acceptability of our words in God's sight is dependent upon them being consistent with what our hearts feel or think. This text urges us to always speak the kind of words that confirm what we believe or think in our hearts about God, His love and His power. We can contradict that belief with careless words from our mouth, and this is not acceptable in God's sight. He wants us to speak to our spouses, words that glorify Him. God didn't accept Cain's offering (Genesis 4:1-7). His offering was faithless and fruitless. So we don't want our speech to be an unacceptable before God. Watch what you say to each other.

DEFILEMENT COMES FROM WITHIN

What you have inside you will eventually come out of your mouth. Is it God's word? If not, what you have stored will come out. In this case, it will be evil words. Out of the abundance of the heart, the mouth speaks. Jesus said, *"These people draw near to me with their mouth, honor me with their lips but their heart is far from me. And in vain they worship me." Mathew 15:7-9.* And he called the Pharisees and Scribes hypocrites. Well we can't worship God with our mouths and at the same time speak evil and quarrel. Our hearts need to be right and to be filled with God's word. Let's work on our hearts, which affects our mouths; so that we glorify God in our relationships.

LISTEN TO YOUR PARTNER

Do you want to be a good partner? Be swift to hear but slow to speak (James 1:19). Become a good listener, don't love talking too much, constantly learn to listen when your partner is talking; especially when they are hurt and they are pouring out their heart. Listen to their complaint in order to make wise decisions. Whatever they say might not be right but first listen and then help bring some light where they are wrong.

It takes wisdom to listen to your partner, and wisdom will make your home godly. If your partner wants you to cut down on your weight, do something about it. If your husband says you need to get some cooking skills, go ahead and take a catering course. If you as the husband have those skills, teach your wife and work together as a team. If it is cleanliness that your wife needs, please work on it. Why not cut down the beard if she doesn't like it? And why don't you clean your house so that your husband looks forward to coming back home?

Next, we will look at some of the causes of conflict in marriage, in the following chapter.

Chapter 15

CAUSES OF CONFLICTS IN MARRIAGE

There are many things that lead to conflicts in marriage. We will look at them in turn, and consider how best to deal with them. I discuss what the Lord has laid on my heart, and share my personal experience, over twenty years I have been married.

MONEY

Jesus is the head of our homes; therefore we must follow biblical teachings about everything, including our finances. In marriage both husband and wives are under obligation to tithe and give offerings. Malachi 3:8-12 reveals what God has to say about it. If you want to see the grace of God in your marriage, always tithe and give offerings. Have a budget and stick no it. Be transparent with each other. Decide who is going to do what. In our home we decided with Peter that he deals with all the major bills, i.e. paying of the mortgage, school fees, and I pay all the other bills, it has worked for us.

We decided that once we set up a budget we will not allow temptations to make us change it. Even if there's a big sale, we ignore it and stick to our budget. Peter is very good in this area.

Are you in debt today? Are your finances in a mess? Don't give up! There's hope for you. You will come out of it, if you admit you went wrong and make the necessary changes to your financial management. I want to encourage you to continue giving with the little you have. Remember God's principle is, give and it will be given back to you, good measure, pressed down, shaken together, and running over... Through your giving, God will deliver your marriage. You will go through the storms in Jesus' name. I decree and declare to you that, you will have a marriage free of discord over money. You will have enough money to meet your monthly expenses. You will have money to save and have a happy marriage, and the zeal of the Lord shall perform it. Amen.

We decided to stop using many credit cards when we almost accumulated a big debt. We only kept two because we knew we would need them once in a while, if we ever came across a rainy day. You don't have to take out a loan if you do not have a repayment plan. Consider how you will generate the money to pay it back? How are you going to pay in time to avoid big interests? Rather than use loans and credit cards to pay for items, why not wait to buy some things, in order to pay with cash, when you can afford to? A lack of financial wisdom can put too much pressure on your marriage. Have a separate account in which you manage your savings. I have noticed that as Christians, we get so carried away in giving towards conferences, missions or seminars, we forget to ask God where He would want us to give. Some believers give without consulting their spouses. This is not right. I don't mean that every time you give you have to consult your partner - no! What I mean is, if God tells you to give something like a car or something you all use in the family, you need to first inform your partner.

Be wise with how you spend. Some men will get tempted to engage in gambling, only to end up in trouble with their families. This can apply to women as well. One time I saw a woman on TV who had ran up expenses on the company credit cards, gambling. She used all her savings and maxed-out every financial resource her family had. She was depressed, and eventually her marriage failed.

What are your financial goals? Do you have to put your money together? Decide what will work for both of you. In our case, Peter has his savings account, but I can access it any time. I also have mine which he can access. Then we have a joint account where we pay the bills. We don't have arguments because we are transparent. The problem comes when a spouse is fearful because the partner is careless with money. A joint account in such a situation is impossible. So you need to discuss your fears and come to a compromise, then implement what works best for both partners.

Some women hide their money. Add to your man's life, don't subtract. Don't be extravagant, spend money wisely. The Bible talks about a notable woman, remarkable, distinguished, prominent, a well to do woman. After discerning that Elisha was a man of God, the woman in 2 Kings 4:8-32 wanted to build him a house on the roof. In those days this was the best place. She chose the best place for the man of God. Even though she had all it takes, she first consulted her husband. She was a wise woman. I don't mean that when you want to do your shopping, first get permission from your husband. However, if you are planning to buy something extravagant, inform him, and seek his advice.

INCOME

Do whatever you can to ensure you both have an income. If your husband has the means to meet all the family's needs and is happy for you to stay home and raise the children, that's fine. Otherwise because of the expenses you have in the family, you will need different sources of incomes. Couples have had problems in their homes where in some cases the wife is not working but spending. I would suggest to a non-working wife that if your husband is financially stretched, it might be high time you looked for a part-time job. It is not biblical to become a burden to your partner. You lose respect and cause your household to suffer. Look for a job, and if need be, study a course that will help you will your work prospects. When your company plans to promote, they will first consider you because of your extra qualifications.

There are many courses you can do especially in the area of IT. Being in the 21st century where knowledge is increasing, we need to wake up. Go and do a computer course. It is an added advantage if you can be computer literate. The Bible says that skill will bring success. Learn the basics like word processing, database, opening and sending e-mails. It will help you when you are looking for a job. This applies to ladies as well as men.

It's important to be computer savvy, for your personal life and leisure; for example, booking a seat on a plane on most airlines nowadays has to be done online. It is a way of simplifying the process and controlling the seating options available on flights. If you don't know how to access all these opportunities you lose out. When you get at the airport these days, they first consider those who already checked in, and the likelihood is you will not be able to have a good seat because those who booked online got first choice with seating options. Once a seat has been chosen by someone, they will not change it. Please wake up, do something about your skills. British Airways for example has all the information you would require by simply accessing ba.com. All these are opportunities for us. If you do a course in IT, when your employer looks for people who will be there to help the customers operate new system; you will be a good candidate for the job. If you're not happy with IT, there other courses you can do. Look for something to do, start a small business, for example. Ask God to give you creative ideas.

DEMANDING

Wives, if you rely on your husband for money, do not be demanding for it. Be patient and present your needs to your God instead of putting pressure on your man. I don't mean you don't tell him your needs. Tell him in a polite way, but if he has no money, to give you leave it to God. We are told, blessed is the person who trusts in the Lord. Your confidence is in God. You will be like a tree planted by the waterside that sends out its roots by the stream (Jeremiah 16:7-8). When you consistently focus your eyes on God, He will bless you and you will not lack any good thing. I have learnt to focus my eyes on God because people have limits, whereas God is unlimited in what He can do for you. Even governments can let you down but God never will. He is an all sufficient God. He is Jehovah Jeireh, God your provider.

Though I have my own money, when my husband gives me some, I feel grateful and I thank him. I was not always like this though. I would act foolishly by complaining if he gave me what I considered little. I would start complaining "that's too little, I need more, I saw money in your wallet; give me more." Until I discovered that I was being too demanding and unrealistic. God rebuked me and I learnt my lesson. Today am a changed woman.

CONTENTMENT

My friend, urge your mate to choose satisfaction over salary. Don't become a workaholic and abandon your family because you lack the ability to be content with what you have. Wise up! It's better to be married to a happy person with a thin wallet, than to a miserable person with a thick one.

'It is better to have little with fear for the Lord than to have great treasure with turmoil' (Proverbs 15:16).

Pursue the virtue of contentment. 'Godliness with contentment is great gain' (1 Timothy 6:6). Money doesn't give you all you need, you must learn to be contented in God. Whoever loves money never has money enough (Ecclesiasts 5:10).

If God blesses you with money after you've learnt to be content in him, then great. Love should be first before money. Money complements love, it should not be a priority. Be careful when choosing or changing jobs. Consult your God; not your greed.

COMMUNICATION

Communication is one of the most basic skills needed in any human relationship. In marriage it is especially important that a couple master this ability. It has been said, "Communication is more than just words. It is tone, gestures, and body language." Ask yourself if your words match with your body language? Lack of communication and poor communication in a home can create problems. Learn to attack the problem instead of attacking your spouse. Poor communication can literally kill your marriage.

The Bible says that little foxes spoil the vine. Learn to communicate well with one another, even in little issues, because in most cases it's through the little issues that we fall out with each other. If these things are not addressed properly, they could cause a crack in the foundation of your relationship. Think about the ways you have handled certain frustrating issues with each other. Pointing fingers and saying, "You always do this or that, or you'll never change this or that" is not proper communication. Alternatively, you could sit down and gently say; "Could you please try to do, or not do, this or that" and "This is why I get upset; and do you understand why?" Then come to some sort of agreement on how to handle the situation in future.

Peter walks away from a big argument to cool off. He will excuse himself and walk away, but after an hour or so, he will call me and say, "I am sorry, forgive me, I am coming back to resolve this issue." One time he called and sung to me, "I just called to say I love you" and then he said, "Darling I wasn't happy about what you said. I forgive you and I am coming so that we can resolve this matter." Because of his humility he has always won my heart. When he comes back, I just sit and listen. After a while I say sorry to him and he does the same and we move on.

Even when something seems obvious to you, don't assume your mate can read your mind. And never resort to 'the silent treatment.' Tell them what's bothering you, even if it means working through a disagreement. It's when you don't care enough to disagree, that you need to worry.

Listening is also communicating. A husband looking through the paper came upon a study that said women use more words than men. Excited to prove to his wife that he had been right all along when he accused her of talking too much, he showed her the study results. It read "Men use about 15,000 words per day, but women use 30,000". The wife thought for a while, then finally she said to her husband "It's because we have to repeat everything we say." The husband said "What?"

When you get to know your partner, it makes life easy. Develop an intimacy that is deeper than sex. Get to know their thoughts, feelings, desires, and dreams as though they were your own. Share them. Grow your dreams together. When problems come up, never raise your voice. It's a sign of disrespect. Voice your objection another way. *"A gentle answer turns away wrath, but harsh words stir up anger."* Proverbs 15:1

Spend more time listening than talking. *"…be quick to listen, slow to speak, and slow to get angry"* James 1:19. Stay teachable. Solomon says, "Answering before listening is…stupid and rude'" Proverbs 18:13. Keep an open mind. Don't form your response while your spouse is still talking. The Bible says, *"Do not merely look out for your own…interests, but also for the interests of others"* Philippians 2:4. Never become so entrenched in your position that you don't consider your partner's viewpoint. It has been said, "Listening is about connecting and acknowledging where the other person's coming from."

Have you seen the t-shirt that says, 'I'm talking and I can't shut up!' I remember when Peter and I were dating each other, we talked for hours. But I realised when I got married, that unless I worked at it, our conversations sometimes became superficial and led us to disagreements. God says, '…be willing to listen and slow to speak…' because there's an art to communicating, dear sisters, let us learn to let our husbands lead. When they're talking about things outside our field of interest, remember, God said, "Submit to one another…" (Ephesians 5:21). Sometimes that means asking your partner, "What do you want to talk about?" Some of us will not even allow our husbands to finish a sentence before we finish it for them! As women of God, we need to wise up.

One day Peter told me, "Can you stop saying, we need to talk" because it feels like you are threatening me; rather, say to me, "Peter, can we talk for a few minutes. This is less threatening." When I thought about it, I realised he was right.

DWELLING ON THE PAST

Develop a communication style that focuses on future problem solving rather than get stuck rehearsing past mistakes. Early in our marriage Peter and I had a bad start and passed through many heart breaking struggles before we finally learnt how to relate effectively to each other. Finally, I did two things and they worked; gradually of course. When you cover a transgression, you seek love, but if you keep repeating a matter, it will strain your friendship (Proverbs 17:9). Where your heart is, there you will be. Lot's wife in the Bible looked back because that's where her heart was. When you continue looking at your past, it means that is where you're heart is. You can never progress in life if all you do is to rewind and replay your past. As a matter of fact, you will become stagnant. When you keep on repeating a matter, it will bring separation between you and your spouse, both physically and spiritually (Proverbs 17:9B).

Move on and try your best to look at the good things your partner has done over the years. Write them somewhere and keep meditating on them. As you do this, it will help you to be appreciative. Paul the apostle set an example for us when he said, one thing he does is to forget those things which are behind and reach forward to those things which are ahead (Philippians 3:13). Remember, in Christ, you are a new creature; old things have passed away; behold, all things have become new. Christ has given you his mind; claim it so that the past will not become bondage to you (2 Corinthians 5:17).

Even if this is your second marriage, forget the past and move on. Yes, you worked hard at it, and I'm sure you sweated for that marriage but please move on for your own good. Be positive about your new marriage. Stop thinking defeat. Stop thinking about negatives; defeat misery, fear and the like. Before you enter marriage, deal with your past. If you do not, you will go into marriage with your issues. If not dealt with, they can paralyse your new relationship. So go before God in prayer and pour out your heart. Even if you are the guilty party, in an earlier break up, you still need to move on. And I hope in your new relationship you can appreciate where God has brought you from. You probably suffered so much; you don't want to go back to the same mess. You didn't get this marriage easily. It should mean a lot to you. You have paid a price for it, so take care of it, and leave the past behind you.

I remember when I was overweight, weighing seventeen stone; I went to see my GP for my regular check up and he advised me to start working out. Now, exercise requires much discipline. It takes the grace of God, and surely God has been good to me. I am now fourteen stone. My target is twelve and I know I will get there, but all in all, it was not easy for me, working out on the treadmill for thirty minutes and then moving on to the other machines. Sometimes I had to call upon God to help me. Reducing my weight was not easy. I paid a price it and now I have to be so serious with what I eat. I have to guard myself against my old eating habits, so I am mindful of what I eat in order to maintain my present size.

The same thing has to happen for you in your marriage. You didn't get this marriage easily. It should mean a lot to you. You have paid a price for it, so take care of it. Work hard, don't grow weary. Your breakthrough will come as you work at it.

In order to put past issues behind you and to effectively lead a new life, it is always better to get professional and emotional support. That extends beyond plain legal advice, and professional Christian counseling. This will become a crucial act of empowerment for you. We can do nothing to change the past, but we can do something to shape the future. If your partner fails you along the way, forgive them. Don't go back and continually bring up the issue, *"He who covers a transgression seeks love, but he who repeats a matter separates friends."* Proverbs 17:9

IN – LAWS

Whoso rewards evil for good, evil shall not depart

from his house. Proverbs 17:13

It takes the grace of God to live and relate with in-laws. Learn to sow good seeds of love in their lives. Shower them with love and you will receive the same love in return. The measure you use will be measured to you, even more (Mark 4:24B). Love covers a multitude of sins. They might not even see or appreciate your love, but don't get discouraged. God will fight on your behalf. If you drive your spouse's family members out, you may also drive your spouse away.

I heard of a story of a lady who, after her wedding day and settling down, asked her husband to get rid of his family members. She reminded him how during courtship he promised her he would rent them a house. He never fulfilled his promise, and so the sister was mad with him and his entire family. The issue got out of hand to the extent that the husband told the wife to leave; after all, 'she had found them together.' I believe the wife in this situation had a valid point at the beginning, although she did not exercise wisdom with how she approached the matter. What she should have done is to pray about it and seek God's guidance. Secondly, she should have reminded her husband of his promise to relocate them. She went overboard by nagging the man to the extent that the in-laws came to learn of it. When you start an argument and dwell on it all the time, you are acting a fool according to the Bible (Proverbs 18:6).

God will give you the right words to tell your husband if the situation gets fom bad to worse; if you seek His guidance. Also we are told in (Proverbs 18:7) when a fool speaks, he is ruining himself; he gets caught in the trap of his own words. Measure your words well before you speak on any a sensitive matter in your marriage. Embrace your in-laws and show them love; be nice to them, even if they don't respond to you in a nice way. In the case we just looked at with the newly-wed wife who did not want to live with her in-laws; by the grace of God, the husband eventually rented a house for the in-laws to live in. The love of God is surely powerful, but it takes patience to get results.

The truth of the matter is that it is hard to live with in-laws, so the best thing to do is to make plans for them, arrange somewhere else for them to stay, and encourage them to get jobs so that they can learn to be independent. Otherwise, they may create a strain on your marriage; especially for newly-weds.

Ruth's testimony with her mother-in law is a big challenge for us; they had a good relationship with each other. *"And Boaz answered and said unto her, It hath fully been showed me, all that thou hast done unto thy mother in law since the death of thine husband: and how thou hast left thy father and thy mother, and the land of thy nativity, and art come unto a people which thou knewest not heretofore. The LORD recompense thy work, and a full reward be given thee of the LORD God of Israel, under whose wings thou art come to trust Ruth." Ruth 2:11-12*

Because of her good behaviour and her attitude towards her mother in-law, Boaz blessed Ruth. Do you think they never had issues? Of course they must have had them, but both of them were wise. They learnt how to live with their differences. Naomi is a good example to mother-in-laws. God expects you to be godly, and not to manipulate your chuildren and their spouses (Ruth 2:18B). Look at what Naomi said about Ruth in Ruth 2:19. Imagine if Ruth had misunderstandings with her mother-in-law, she would have discouraged Boaz to marry Ruth. Treat your in-laws well, and God who is in heaven will reward you.

A friend of mine had problems with her mother-in-law. She couldn't stand her. Her husband was too close to his mother and it seemed like her mother-in-law would have been happy for these two to divorce. But the husband loved her a great deal. Sometimes this friend of mine would hear her husband tell his mum, how much he loved his wife; how important she was to him. The mother-in-law would back off but after a period of time, she would come back to bring

꧁꧂
"TIME SPENT
QUARRELLING IS TIME
STOLEN FROM
ROMANCE."
-ROBERT KAYANJA-

misunderstandings. I advised my friend to pray for her and just shower her with love. It didn't work straight away. It took years. Nothing changed and she still made nasty little digs about her daughter-in-law.

It was not easy for my friend to stay with her husband because her mother-in-law was doing all in her power to tear the marriage apart. Because he saw everything his wife was doing for his mum. My friend was lucky, because some husbands normally side with their mothers. God vindicated her. Her husband proved how much he cared about his wife and this made her mother-in-law mad.

I advised my friend to also show her husband how much she appreciated his efforts to reassure, in order to reassure him of her love. Although his mum was an ogre, I told her to be the bigger person. Finally, with the help of God and the wisdom God gave me to give her, she won the battle. Today they are happily married. Her mother-in-law gave up! She is settled in her home and no longer pocks her nose into her son's marriage.

I read a true story of a daughter in-law and her mother-in-law that moved me to tears. Just two years after their marriage, her husband, brought the idea of asking his mother to move from the village and spend her remaining years with them. Her father-in-law had passed away while he was still very young and his mother had endured much hardship and struggled on her own to provide for him, right up to him completing his university degree. "You could say that she suffered a great deal and did everything you could expect a woman to do to bring him to where he is today." She immediately agreed and started preparing the spare room.

When the mother-in-law came, she brought all her habits and lifestyle with her. For example, when the lady of the house would buy flowers to decorate the sitting room, the mother in law would have none of it. She would comment "I do not know how you young people spend your money, what do you buy flowers for? You cannot eat flowers." She would ask how much they cost every time her daughter–in-law bought them. Whenever I came back from the market, she would also ask me how much each thing costs. She would then continue to grumble away. Her husband would say "Just don't tell her the full price of everything. That will solve the problem." That was the beginning of the friction to an otherwise happy life style. "Mother hated it most when my husband would wake up to prepare breakfast," she once remarked.

At the table, her mother-in-law's facial expression

would always be like the dark clouds before a thunderstorm, and my friend would pretend not to notice. Her husband started acting funny, how ever much she tried to act cute, he totally ignored her. She got mad and asked him, "What wrong did I do?" He stared at her and said, "Can you just give in to her once? Time passed, but her mother-in-law never spoke to her and there was a very awkward feeling hanging in the house. In this period of cold war, her husband was caught in a dilemma as to who to please, his wife or his mother. In order to stop her son from having to prepare breakfast, she took the important task of preparing breakfast without any prompting. "At the breakfast table, she would look at her son happily eating his breakfast and cast that reprimanding stare at me for having failed to perform my duty as a wife."

To avoid the embarrassing breakfast situation, she stopped having breakfast at home. One night, while in bed, her husband was a little upset and asked her, "Is it because you think that mum's cooking is not clean that you chose not to eat at home? "He turned his back on me and left me alone in tears, as feelings of unfairness overwhelmed me." After some time he said, "Okay, just for me, can you have breakfast at home?" I was left with no choice but to do as he had said.

The next morning she was having porridge prepared by her mother and she felt a sudden churn in her stomach and everything inside seemed to be rushing up her throat. She tried to suppress the urge to throw up but she couldn't. She threw down the bowl rushed to the bathroom and vomited everything out. Just as she was catching her breath, she saw her mother-in-law crying and grumbling very loudly in her language. Her husband was standing at the bathroom doorway staring at her with fire burning in his eyes. She opened her mouth but no words cam, "I really did not mean it she said." They had their big fight that day; her mother-in-law took a look at us, then stood up and slowly made her way out of the house as my husband followed. For three days, her hubby did not return home, not even a phone call.

She had been trying her best to put up with her. For no reason, she simply had no appetite for food, and coupled with all the events happening at home, she was at the lowest point in her life. Her colleagues at work said, "You look terrible; you should go and see a doctor." The doctor confirmed that she was pregnant. Now it became clear to her why she threw up that fateful morning; a sense of sadness floated through that otherwise happy news. "Why didn't mother who had been through this before, think of the possibility of this being the reason that day?" When she went for a maternity check-up in hospital, she saw her husband standing there. It had only been 3 days, but he looked fatigued. He pretended that he didn't know her. He had that disgusted look in his eyes that cut right through her heart.

She went back home and lay on the bed thinking about him and the disgusted look in his eyes, that night. The sound of the drawers opening woke her up. She switched on the lights and she saw her husband with tears rolling down his face. He was removing some money. She stared at him in silence; he ignored her, took some money and left the house. The next day, she did not go to work. She wanted to clear this up and have a good talk with him. When she went to his office, his secretary gave her a wired look and said, "His mother had an accident and she is now in the hospital." She stood there in shock. She rushed to the hospital and by the time she got there, she had already passed away. Her husband's face was expressionless. She couldn't control the tears in her eyes. My God, How could this happen? Throughout the funeral, her husband did not say a single word to her, he gave the occasional stare. She only managed to find out brief facts about the accident from other people. On the fateful day, her mother-in-law left her house, and walked confused towards the bus park, apparently intending to go back to her house in the village. As her husband came after her, she tried to walk faster and as she tried to cross the street faster, a taxi came and hit her.

She finally understood how much her husband must hate her. "Indirectly, I had killed his mother." My husband moved into another room and came home every night smelling of alcohol. And she would be buried under the guilt and self pity. She could hardly breathe. She wanted to explain to him; tell him that they were going to have their baby soon, but each time, I saw the dead look in his eyes; all the words she had at the brink of her mouth just fell back in.

As the days went by, her hubby came home late. One day, as she passed a food store, looking into the glass window, she saw her husband and a girl sitting facing each other. She understood what it meant. After recovering from the moment of shock, she entered the restaurant, stood in front of him and stared hard at him, not a tear in her eyes. She had nothing to say to him, and there was no need to say anything. "The girl looked at me, looked at him and stood to leave but he stretched out his hand and stopped her. That night he did not come home." He had chosen to use that as a way to indicate to her that that was the end of their marriage.

He did not come home anymore after that. Sometimes, when she returned home from work she could tell that the wardrobe had been touched. Because of a fatal misunderstanding, the person who loved her the most in this world, was gone forever.

Endless cruel misunderstandings disrupted the blissful footsteps in this family. Their original intention of having mother enjoy some quiet and peaceful moments in her remaining years with them went terribly wrong, and at such a high price. Let what happened to this family teach us. I pray that this will not be our potion with our in-laws, in Jesus' name. May the Lord God give us the wisdom and grace to support our in-laws and love them, in Jesus' name!

SHARING INTERESTS

You find a family where each member has their favorite player on a football, cricket or tennis. Suppose they are watching football and it becomes a problem! In my home my husband is a supporter of the Chelsea football team, and my sons and I support Arsenal. My daughter has no interest in football. She prefers watching other programs like American idol and America's next top model. I used to not be interested in football, but I discovered that it is important to support each other's interests. It can help to support your relationships. If your man is a phlegmatic you can show an interest by allowing him to speak. Husbands; don't force your wives to support your club. Rather, encourage her to just sit there and watch with you, and wives; be supportive even if you're bored. It will help both of you to catch up with each other, and to build your relationship.

When football is on I sit there and watch with dad and the boys. When Arsenal scores; we scream together. I have now developed an interest. Guess what happens?

When Arsenal and Chelsea play, I don't take sides. I just sit and watch. We just watch and enjoy as a family. I heard a story of a man that beat up his wife because she was not supporting his team. It became so serious that they had to separate. Another couple had a serious argument about the elections; because the wife and husband were supporting different political parties. After a long period of time, their friends had to sit them down and reconcile them, but it was not easy.

My boys have taught me about premiership charts and tables so that I understand what team is in the lead, who can beat who, etc? Now, I know when Everton is playing, or West Ham, etc. When Lillian, my daughter, is watching American idol, I go and watch with her for a short while and afterwards I go onto do my own stuff.

Some of us are so spiritual; we don't want to watch anything, and would prefer to just listen to gospel music and watch gospels channels. What is your favorite program on TV apart from the gospel channels? Have you tried watching biographies of successful people in life? You can learn from them. Or how about business programmes and news channels? Do you have a favourite sport? What is your favorite team? Don't be over spiritual; it is important to be balanced.

A wife should get to know her husband's interests. It might be Tennis. Can you imagine his friends come to your home and start chatting about Tennis, and you have nothing to contribute! He may take an interest in current news, and you never sit down to watch with him. You can't contribute anything. You will look and feel awkward. If it's Tennis he likes, get to know some information about it, like, know about the best players. Compare them as you talk in your conversations, for example "Jamie Murray and Andy who is your best player?" "By the way, remind me are these players from Scotland and Britain?" This makes a difference; it will cause your man to talk and open up.

Husbands also need to know their wives' interests. It could be watching geographical channels, History channels, driving around, or going to watch movies at the cinemas. Go out of your way and please her. I love watching news, and always encourage my husband to sit and we watch it with me, though he prefers catching up with the news on internet. He is into gadgets, but still sits down and we watch it together.

I do a lot of reading, aside from the Bible. I read news papers, Christian books and magazines. I read the good things and leave out the bad stuff. As I read, my husband keeps on asking me what I am reading and I read for him, so that we can share our interest.

It has been said, "Winners of arguments never always win, because consistent losers never forget."

CHILDREN

Never allow the children to cause a rift between the two of you. Women tend to have this problem, especially on issues involving children, they tend to side with 'their' children. It gets worse when dad and mum have an argument and mum draws the children in, to help fight her cause. It is better to keep them out of arguments.

If these conflicts are not dealt with quickly, they can cause divorce. Everyday remember to ask God for more supernatural grace to enable you to live a happy marriage. Everyday, when I wake up, I ask for more grace from God to come upon my family and marriage. And surely, I have seen God do it. Believe it and release God's grace and anointing into your marriage. Many people say marriage is hard nowadays. If this is the way you think, then of course it will be difficult for you. However, if you are a solid Christian who knows your God very well, then God will give you His anointing so that you find marriage easier because the anointing destroys every yoke. Do you feel like giving up? Don't because you have believed in God and His anointing and grace. You will see a change gradually. And when you pray, wait patiently for God's intervention. You may not see a change straight away, but it will come. The problem we have is that many people or couples want to see change quickly. They want to see results without having to make any effort of consistent praying and consistent forgiving. You ask yourself, 'When will my partner ever change?' Change will come when you stop nagging, complaining, being forceful, and when you learn keep a good attitude.

Complaining that your partner is not changing will not change anything. Make adjustments first and your spouse will change. Do your part by putting strife out of your marriage, and God will bless you and your union. A house divided continually is brought to destruction. It might not happen straight away, but if you continue allowing strife in your marriage, then down the road, destruction will come.

God wants to see how hard you are prepared to press on. Show God that you are patient, pray and believe, his word and then He will give you grace to endure and enjoy your marriage even when there are problems. If you expect everything to work itself out on its own, and think you can just sit back and rest, I can guarantee you; you will not see God's grace and favour in your marriage. Not everything can be attained easily with God's grace alone. Don't sit and relax, waiting for your marriage to somehow work out. No! The kingdom of

God is taken by violence. Pray, fast, and love unconditionally; and then you will see a difference in your marriage. As I say this I don't mean that if you have domestic violence in your marriage you shield just call on God's grace and wait. No! This is a different issue; we don't want you dead, we want you alive. If there's domestic violence in your marriage and you have prayed and have seen no results, go quickly to your pastor or Christian counsellor before it's too late.

LACK OF BALANCING

The last conflict I want to look at is what I call a lack of balancing your career and your family. Many ministers of God, and some couples, need to have an established order in their families. It is important to give quality time to your family. I always give my family time, and I never put my church ministry before my family. I don't allow ministry to put my family under pressure. If you are involved in ministry do not take the problems of the church home with your. You need to enjoy your time at home or else you and your family will be stressed out. Never allow the weight of ministry to bear on your family. This has caused divorce in marriages, and has made some children to backslide. You cannot win the whole world and lose your family. Let everything be done decently and in order, according to 1 Corinthians 14:40.

Bring order in your family. There are cases when in addition to the husband the wife is also in ministry. In this instance she will definitely get to know about the problems. But in cases where one partner is in the five-fold ministry and the other is not, avoid bringing too much ministry baggage home.

If God has called the husband as a pastor, it doesn't necessarily mean He has called the wife to be the co-pastor or vice versa. I don't deny the fact that God can call them that way. Of course He can! There are so many men and women of God that are called to work together as husband and wife and that is fine. But did you know that there are partners that just make their spouses pastors, when actually it's their idea, not God's plan? This is not right. It will cause problems in the church and in your home.

Then there are some partners who hinder their spouses from serving God. They discourage them and in some cases threaten to leave them if they state a desire to go and serve God. This is very dangerous. Whether husband or wife, you cannot stand in the way of God, or else you risk losing your life and marriage. Some husbands think the only place for their wives is at home and in the kitchen. Your wife is called and was created with purpose. What right do you have to stop your wife from serving her God? And wives, what right do you have to stop your man from serving his

God? Do you know that you will have to give an account on judgement day? Men, you are not above God, you may be the head of your home but you don't have the right to hinder your wife from serving God.

THE BUILDER

God is the builder of marriage. Every couple needs to understand that it is not them building it. That is why when you are in conflict; the best thing to do is to go to God in prayer and seek His advice. For God to build your marriage, you have to understand that it is not you building your marriage in your own wisdom, it is God orchestrating the building process. This scripture says, "Unless the Lord builds the house they labour in vain that build it" (Psalms 127:1-2). You need to come to that point where you are not able to build anything yourself. The Lord is the one who is able to build your marriage. Don't only rely on your prayers and experience but make sure you always have that special relationship with God. He is the only one who can build your marriage. Take your marriage to Him in prayer so that He can build it, restore, and revive it. Always put your confidence in God, in His mercy and grace that are new every morning.

Don't ever put your whole trust in prayer and fasting, except if you do it knowing that ultimately, your faith is in none other than God Almighty. Prayer and fasting are important. After all, it is the effective, fervent prayer of a righteous man that avails much. However, your reliance on prayer should not divert your faith in the direction of human effort or a reliance on your personal works. You must make a distinction between trusting God and trusting your prayers. It's not by might nor by power, but by God's Spirit that good things happen (Zechariah 4:6).

Your efforts do not play the decisive role. All decisions are taken by the Holy Spirit. Don't rely on your own strength or on the help of man. Rather, look up to God who builds your marriage, and rely on His mercies and His goodness. You need to come to that point, where you are not able to build anything yourself. It's the work of God. Are you a lawyer or a judge? Your law in itself, without God's power cannot solve marital problems. It is God who will give a couple mutual understanding so that they can solve their issues.

Sit and solve the problems together and take your marriage to Him in prayer; to the one who never fails. Always put your confidence in God, putting your trust in His mercy and grace. May God's grace flow in your marriage, and may you rely on His mercies and His goodness. I release the anointing of the Holy Spirit on your marriage. And I speak healing in your hearts, in Jesus' name.

Chapter 16

GRACE EVERYDAY

"Now the multitude of those who believed were of one heart and one soul; neither did anyone say that any of the things he possessed was his own, but they had all things in common. And with great power the apostles gave witness to the resurrection of the Lord Jesus. And great grace was upon them all." Acts 4:32-33

Much grace was upon the early church and here is the reason why! They worked together; their souls and hearts were knitted together. The weak and the strong complemented each other and more grace was given to them. Do you want more grace in your life, in your marriage, in your business? Work together as a team! Forgive one another and don't magnify small issues into a big issue. If your spouse doesn't say thank you for something you did, do not turn it into a national crisis. Don't focus on each other's weaknesses; rather focus on the strong areas you have.

Has he not paid the bill on time? If not, don't make a

war in your house. So he has made a mistake, we all do; move on. Two wrongs do not make a right. Give him the benefit of doubt. Husbands ought to show the same understanding to their wives. In marriage you need to have a good attitude, and not allow one mistake to steal your joy. Grow in the Grace of God. Sometimes my husband Peter annoys me immensely but I have come to discover that God himself allows it. The worse in other people will bring out the worse in us. This gives us an opportunity to grow spiritually and to work on our character. The Bible says "iron sharpens iron" Your spouse is the sand paper of the Holy Spirit; the Lord will use them as a sand paper to rub away your character flaws, so that the good in you can shine. Just learn how to cry out for more Grace everyday.

If you want to prosper in your relationship and you truly want peace? If so, learn to bite your tongue and stay calm when you have disagreement with your spouse, or they do something you don't like. We are told in 3 John 1:2 to prosper in all things - marriage included. God wants you to prosper in all areas of your life.

I have learnt that I need the grace of God every day in my marriage. I remember when every day I would argue with Peter, there was no peace in our home. I would feel frustrated, confused thoughts would run in my mind saying, "why don't you call it quits?" Of course I knew that was the devil. The going got so tough; I broke down in tears and pleaded with God. I heard the Holy Spirit speak to me, "Josephine, ask me for more grace every day. I have sufficient grace for you." Wow! It was an eye opener for me. I started asking for His grace and it has worked for me, to this day. It does not matter how rough the going gets, keep asking for more grace and please have faith that you have received it.

FAITH

Faith and grace go together. Even if you have faith that moves mountains, if you don't understand the grace of God, it will not work. Faith is like a computer. For a computer to work you have to switch the power on. The equivalent of that power is grace. In order to get our needs met, or receive anything from the Lord, we must have both faith and grace. "It is by grace through faith that we are saved." Sometimes faith fails as in the case of Mark 9:17-24 "Help my unbelief." In this example we see that the grace of God had to be relied upon. Just admit it to God when you feel you have no faith at all. God is faithful, He will help you.

"Faith comes by hearing, and hearing by the word of God." Romans 10:17. You have to read and listen to

God's word to increase your faith. The more you hear, the more it goes into your heart. Take time to meditate on it. If you have 'made' it in life, just remember, you wouldn't be where you are today, had it not been for faith. Faith comes to you by what you hear; the word of God that activates your faith, when you step out on it, you receive your breakthrough. Faith causes you to be proactive with what you have heard. I have been in situations where I started to get frustrated about the arguments I had with Peter. I tried to figure out what to do to solve my dilemma. The more I tried the more I got confused, upset and frustrated. I felt I didn't have faith to receive more grace because of the things I had done, but the Holy Spirit would remind me to rely on Him. Trust in God, rely on Him alone. Merriam Webster dictionary defines relying to mean committing or placing in one's care, to place confidence, to be confident. So even if you have failed in some area of your marriage, and you don't feel faith within you, just encourage yourself in God. After all, we shouldn't rely on our feelings, they are not stable. Lean on God. God has always made a way for us in the hard times, and given us grace day by day.

Child of God, God's favour is available to you today! But just because He promises it does not necessarily mean you will experience it automatically. Many things are available to us that we do not enjoy. Why? Because we do not activate our faith in order to receive them!

Favour is actually a form of grace. The word grace and the word favour both come from the same Greek word Charis. So, the grace of God is the favour of God, and His favour causes things to happen that we couldn't make happen, earn or deserve ourselves. When you ask someone for a favour, you are usually asking for that person to do something that they don't have to do. Well, the good news is, at the cross, Jesus paid for and made available all the favor you will ever need. So exercise your faith and ask Him for it! God's grace is receivable (Romans 4:4-5).

There are times I felt like trying to sort out my issues without telling God about it, and the Lord told me that when I try to do things in my own way, I allow pride to come in. Go to God in prayer and tell Him how you feel about your spouse. If you depend on your own abilities or effort and live out God's limitless power of the Holy Sprit, you are going to find yourself in trouble (Zech 4:4-6).

Seek His grace. It is the very thing you need to build and maintain a successful marriage.

Chapter 17

GRACE TURNS FAILURES INTO FERTILIZERS

DIVORCE

When we are talking about divorce, I believe we must include grace. God is not a law master who wants to forcefully bring His people into broken submission. God is very forgiving and loving. He wants His people to experience joy and fulfillment in their lives and this can only be done in the grace of forgiveness. Jesus bore all your sins, and that includes the sin of divorce. All wrongs have been paid for. God's grace will turn your failures into fertilizers as long as you allow Him to work on you and heal you.

Some theologians say that the Bible gives no grounds for divorce or remarriage. Others suggest that the Bible allows for divorce under some circumstances but does not allow for remarriage. Some say that if a divorce is justified, so is the possibility of remarriage. Still others say that God's primary concern is our happiness.

As a pastor, I have been involved in counselling couples with scores of divorce situations. Sometimes, as in cases of extreme mental or physical abuse, my desire is to see a woman become freed from the terror of an abusive husband or vice versa. Yet, I am always uneasy advising on action that has no clear biblical grounds for divorce and remarriage.

Not only did I want to help the abused wife, I also want to help the abusive husband overcome his problem. Transforming lives is more preferable than divorce action that would divide children, friends, and family assets.

The number of people choosing to get married is lower than ever in present times. The decline could be due to rising numbers of children seeing their parents go through divorce. Secondly, research showed new rules in the UK discouraging 'some marriages' have helped produce the lowest rates since figures were first computed in 1862. Since the Act, we have seen marriages drop by more than 50 percent. This situation is very disappointing. It exposes the devil's plan to destroy the institution of marriage. First of all there's need for parents to set an example for their children. Divorce is not the answer to marital problems. In marriage, when you have issues, don't rush into divorce as a solution. Try to work out your differences. Of course there are couples who have divorced because of sound reasons, but God hates divorce. For this reason alone, we should not allow ourselves to entertain the idea. The second issue we looked at that has caused fewer people to getting married is the desire for people to get into marriage for the wrong motives. It is a pity that people only want convenient marriages, which in the end will make them feel guilty.

The emotional and financial cost of divorce and the effect it has on children alone, should discourage couples from getting divorced. Before you even think of divorcing it is better that you go to see Christian counsellors and ask them to help you reconcile. A couple was planning to divorce and decided to see a Christian counsellor. When I next met them they told me, after the fifth session with the counsellor, they were better informed about the effects of divorce and so they didn't see it as being the answer to their problems. Today they are still living together; God is gradually healing their relationship. Some people say they are not compatible and that's why they divorce. My question to such people usually is, since when did you find out? Because before you get married to someone you have to be in courtship; and that is when you get to know each other.

It's easy to think that only "other people" get divorced. That your own marriage is somehow immune to troubles, infidelity and fights. After all, how many of us would walk down the aisle if we believed our relationships would end up in divorce?

Believe me or not, no relationship comes with a lifetime guarantee. Even men and women who grew up in stable homes, who attend church and consider themselves Christians, who promise "till death do us part," can have it all fall apart.

Although God permits divorce under certain circumstances, it's never His ideal. One couple, I counselled, who worked through their marriage troubles said, "We're glad we didn't give up during the difficult years. We hung in long enough to realise that it really can get better with time." By committing to work on the relationship, no matter how things ultimately end up, you'll never regret your efforts. As Christians, we know that applying biblical principles to marriage will give us a stronger foundation than those of our unbelieving friends and neighbours.

In Britain today, children are being exposed to family breakdown because the government is undermining marriage; a Tory policy group claimed. A survey of 15,000 mothers found that children are five times more likely to experience family breakdown if their parents are not married.

Divorce will affect your children negatively. They are often used as amunition by the feuding parents whose only interest is to cause as much pain as possible to their now-estranged lovers; in order to seek revenge for what they have felt themselves. What they don't realise is, whenever a weapon is fired, the ammunition doesn't just destroy its target; the ammunition itself gets destroyed. Job writes, '…there is hope for a tree: If it is cut down, it will sprout again, and its new shoots will not fail. Its roots may grow old in the ground and its stump die in the soil, yet at the scent of water it will bud and put forth shoots like a plant' (Job 14:7-9).

Job says that a new shoot can grow out of a dead stump. Please don't destroy the shoot because you've lost the stump! Your destiny is in your seed. If you lose your children, you cut off your future. God has entrusted them to you. You are rich and you are blessed because you have them. Perhaps you cannot save the relationship, but if you cannot or will not, at least save the children. They don't deserve to become casualties of your war. In the midst of your pain, stop and realise that you have a child who needs you, a child entrusted to your care. Providing food and shelter is very good; but don't forget the importance of love, and stability, and spiritual guidance. Without these things, your pain can become their life-long pain. Don't let that happen – save the children!

After a marriage conference, a lady came to me and told me a sad story of her dear sister who lived in Tanzania. She patiently endured a heavy drinking, sexually immoral husband for 7 years, during which she twice contracted a sexually transmitted disease. He had professed faith in Christ shortly before they were married, attended church with her for a short time, and then went back to his old ways. In the end she said her sister divorced him.

Divorce is rampart even among ministers today. This has saddened my heart and what a reproach this has been to the body of Christ. Friends, I want to use this opportunity to encourage you, especially those of us in ministry, to continue to pray for fellow ministers. There is nothing too hard for our God to do even though it might seem like the eleventh hour. Pray for ministers throughout the nations, as we seek to explain to members of our congregations who ask, "How can these things happen among Christian leadership?" This is not time to be judgmental and critical but to pray and stand in the gap for our fellow ministers.

IS DIVORCE BIBLICAL?

The Pharisees also came to Him, testing Him, and saying to Him, "Is it lawful for a man to divorce his wife for just any reason?" He said to them, "Moses, because of the hardness of your hearts, permitted you to divorce your wives, but from the beginning it was not so. And I say to you, whoever divorces his wife, except for sexual immorality, and marries another, commits adultery; and whoever marries her who is divorced commits adultery." Matthew. 19:8.

Because of the hardness of men's hearts, Moses allowed divorce. In the process, however, God provided guidelines. A man had to obtain a certificate of divorce and give it to the unwanted wife. The divorce certificate would show that the woman had been legally released from marriage and that she was now free to marry another.

"And it came to pass, that when Jesus had finished these sayings, He departed from Galilee, and came into the coasts of Judea beyond Jordan; And great multitudes followed him; and he healed them there. The Pharisees also came unto him, tempting him, and saying unto him, Is it lawful for a man to put away his wife for every cause? And he answered and said unto them, Have ye not read, that he which made them at the beginning made them male and female, And said, For this cause shall a man leave father and mother, and shall cleave to his wife: and they twain shall be one flesh? Wherefore they are no more twain, but one flesh. What therefore God hath joined together, let not man put asunder. They say unto him, Why did Moses then command to give a writing of divorcement, and to put her away? He

saith unto them, Moses because of the hardness of your hearts suffered you to put away your wives: but from the beginning it was not so. And I say unto you, Whosoever shall put away his wife, except it be for fornication, and shall marry another, committeth adultery: and whoso marrieth her which is put away doth commit adultery. His disciples say unto him, If the case of the man be so with his wife, it is not good to marry." Mathew 19:10-19

However, the Greek word translated "marital unfaithfulness" is a word which can mean any form of sexual immorality. It can mean fornication, prostitution or adultery, etc. I believe Jesus meant that divorce is permissible if sexual immorality is committed. Sex is such an integral part of the marital bond, "The two will become one flesh." (Genesis 2:24; Matthew 19:5; Ephesians 5:31). Therefore, a breaking of that bond by sexual relations outside of marriage might be a permissible reason for divorce. If so, I also believe Jesus has remarriage in mind in this passage. The phrase "and marries another" (Matthew 19:9) indicates that divorce and remarriage are allowed in an instance of the exception clause, whatever it is interpreted to be.

I want you to notice that only the innocent party is allowed to remarry. Although it is not stated in the text, the allowance for remarriage after a divorce is God's mercy for the one who was sinned against, not for the one who committed the sexual immorality. There may be instances where the "guilty party" is allowed to remarry - but no such concept is taught in this text.

A careful study of Bible passages dealing with divorce makes clear a principle that we can apply: Whenever a divorce occurs on grounds God has declared valid, that divorce carries with it the right of remarriage. Recently a young mother was murdered with her baby daughter in a violent attack by her ex-lover. The ex-lover was a drug addict who later killed himself. The woman's throat was cut and the child was strangled. Do you know these murders could have been prevented if the woman had been given counsel to leave this abusive man?

From the words of Jesus in Matthew 19, and from Paul in 1 Corinthians 7:15, I found only two grounds upon which God sanctions divorce: sexual immorality and the desertion of a believer by an unbeliever. This raises the question, "Is divorce wrong under all other circumstances? What about abuse? Must a woman continue to live with a man who is beating her, and sexually abusing her, or both?

There is no verse in the Bible specifically stating that a woman in an abusive marriage has a right to obtain a divorce. Nor is there any mention of a legal separation. Many pastors and other Christian leaders have gone through great emotional and mental turmoil when confronted with situations of extreme cruelty. I know I have. And in my searching of the Scriptures, I have found a principle that I believe we can apply in such situations. It has permitted me to advise some women to seek a divorce even when the husband was a professing Christian and free from sexual immorality.

GET UP

I don't encourage divorce, it is against the word of God, but if you are already divorced, it already happened, so don't feel judged. I don't know what happened in your marriage, all I can do is to encourage you to get up and be strengthened in the name of Jesus. Did you know you have something to offer to the body of Christ? As long as you have forgiven your partner, be assured that there is hope for you. Allow the fire you have gone through to purify you. A new anointing will be established in your life. And since you have suffered the pain of divorce, your experience will help you to identify with others who are suffering in the same way. Your own hurt will enable you to effectively minister to others. After divorce you may feel lonely at times and consider that you need a new partner. But it's better to allow at least a year before making another serious commitment. You will need time to go through the progress of healing.

Author, Bob Gas once said "It is the broken who become masters at mending." Forget your broken past. Don't let people judge you. They don't know your story.

As Christians, we shouldn't take sides when couples divorce; you don't know who did what. Instead we should pray for them to be forgiven, and if possible, to believe that God can restore them. "He heals the broken-hearted and binds up their wounds" (Psalms 47:3). Why do we disqualify people who are divorced? Leave them to God. It's by the grace of God that you're married. You who are judging also have issues in your own marriage. Set the pretence aside and stop behaving as if you never have problems in your own marriage.

Too often we only share the good side of our marriages; so when others hear, they get discouraged by our one-sided, rosey story. They think that while they are suffering, we have arrived. When we send false messages, we fail to be real and therefore become ineffective at helping others. If we become real with other people, it will help them to hang in there with their own marriages. Challenged couples will be able to say that "If so and so went through this and their marriage survived, I will also succeed." Let us learn to be real and testify, in order to help others. The angels of God overcame Satan by the blood of the lamb and the word of their testimony. The church must not reject divorced people but instead embrace and receive them. Who will receive them if we won't? We gossip and stab them in their backs, forgetting that when Adam and Eve fell, God covered their nakedness. How about us doing the same? Love covers all sins (Psalms 18)

We can forgive the drunkards, murderers and liars, but when it comes to the divorced, we are often too judgmental. A person who has realised their sin and seeks to be forgiven, ought to be forgiven, unconditionally. But if someone divorces, remains arrogant and is not ready to repent, that's a different story. Yet still, such a person merits prayer. Let's accept our brothers and sisters by receiving them back into the field (Ephesians 1: 6). Are you in this situation? God's grace is sufficient for you (2 Corinthians 12: 8-9).

"The woman saith unto him, Sir, give me this water, that I thirst not, neither come hither to draw. Jesus saith unto her, Go, call thy husband, and come hither. The woman answered and said, I have no husband. Jesus said unto her, Thou hast well said, I have no husband: For thou hast had five husbands; and he whom thou now hast is not thy husband: in that saidst thou truly." John 4:15:18

This woman had lived through five failed marriages, I believe she became the talk of the town. She had lost her dignity, had a bad history, was written off, never trusted anyone and was without any self worth. Imagine this is the same woman that Jesus came and spoke to. God's grace visited her. Bob Gas once said that "God's grace turns the failures of our past into fertilizers." When God's grace visits you, he will give you beauty for ashes, a garment of praise in exchange for the spirit of heaviness. Jesus, our great physician, healed a wounded heart. He took away her past and gave her a new hope. Through this woman, the whole town was transformed. God will do it for you as well.

Many divorced people that we counsel struggle with confidence and identity because of what people say about them, and their situation. Don't allow anyone to predict your future. God does not consult your past when He is deciding to bless your future. "Failure is not an event but an opinion." See what the Bible says, *"For a righteous man may fall seven times and rise again..." Proverbs 24:16.*

We are not given this woman's name but we understand that she had divorced five times; a promiscuous woman with a bad reputation and a live-in boyfriend. Listen my friend, when others are looking at your past, Jesus has His eye on your future. With Him every weed is a potential rose! Whatever you've done, God's not holding it against you. Jesus didn't see this woman as bad; He saw her as lost. Big difference! Once she was 'found', she was the kind of person who would be as strong for God as she had been for the devil. This woman was destined to shake up the entire city of Samaria, *"Many of the Samaritans from that town believed in Him because of the woman's testimony..." John 4:39.*

ARE YOU LOOKING FOR GOD? DO YOU HAVE A PERSONAL RELATIONSHIP WITH JESUS CHRIST?

You have seen what God can do. He wants you to come into your heart. You didn't read this book accidentally, it was a divine appointment. You are here for a divine purpose. Would you like to ask Jesus Christ to be Lord and Saviour of your life? Why not read the following Bible verses:

John 3:16 "For God so loved the world that he gave His only Son, that whoever believes in Him shall not perish but have eternal life."

John 14:6 "I am the way the truth and the life. No one comes to the Father except through me."

Acts 10:43 "Everyone who believes in Him receives forgiveness of sins through His name."

If you have believed these words then you need to take the next step by responding to God so that you can receive the gift that He offers. You can do so today! Firstly, you need to say two things to God:

Sorry: You need to ask God to forgive you all that you have done wrong and turn from everything that you know is wrong in your life. The Bible calls this 'repentance'

ASK: You need to invite Jesus to come into your life as Saviour and ask Him to fill you with His Holy Spirit.

SAY THIS SIMPLE PRAYER NOW:

Lord Jesus I am sorry for the things l have done wrong in my life. I ask for your forgiveness and now turn from everything which l know is wrong. Thank you for dying on the cross for me to set me free from my sins. Please come into my life and fill me with your Holy Spirit and be with me forever. Thank you.

If you have made this commitment, we would love to hear from you and be able to help you get established in your new relationship with God. Please write to us, giving your full names, address and age group.

For any further information, please contact us by phone, post or email.

United Kingdom

Pastor Josephine Kyambadde
Latter Rain Ministries International
Unit 8 centre way Montagu Road
Edmonton, London, UK
N9 OAP

Email: latterrainjp@yahoo.co.uk

USA

1629 K Street.
NW suite 300 Washington, DC 2006
Tel: +1 571 201 2948

Uganda

Books available in all major book shops

ABOUT THE AUTHOR

After being dramatically converted and healed of cancer, Pastor Josephine was called to the ministry. She and her husband co-founded Latter Rain Ministries International based in North London, Edmonton. They also have apostolic oversight of churches in Uganda.

They are also co-founders of Fight for families and Marriage Ministry, through their *"Rekindle your Love"* conferences and seminars many marriages have been restored and first love rekindled.

Josephine is the president and founder of Mission in Action Ministries International and President of Woman of Action Ministries International, a non- denominational body. Through her school of *"The Balanced woman,"* Women have learnt to strike a balance spiritually and in their daily lives.

"Dishonest scales are an abomination to the Lord, But a just weight is His delight." Proverbs 11:11 NKJV

She is also one of the directors of Total Woman ministries International, an inter-denominational ministry based in the UK and Co-director of Women Working and Winning together in USA.

She has preached at several seminars and conferences in Europe, USA and at crusades in Africa.

She is a counselor by professional; she holds a first class degree in ministry, a first class diploma in Theology and a diploma in Business Studies.

She is a gifted teacher, motivator, and an author and with grace she preaches the word of God with boldness, the Lord confirming His word. She is the author of *"Woman you are great, In my darkest hour and Mum and Dad wake up"* She has been in ministry for fifteen years and has been married for twenty years. They are blessed with three children Lillian, Derrick and Davis.

AVAILABLE NOW!

TO PURCHASE THESE GROUND BREAKING BOOKS CONTACT

**LATTER RAIN MINISTRIES INTERNATIONAL
UNIT 8 CENTRE WAY MONTAGU ROAD
EDMONTON, LONDON N9 0AP**

**EMAIL: LATTERRAINJP@YAHOO.CO.UK OR INFO@MIAMIK.ORG
WEBSITEWWW.MIAMIK.ORG**

OR TELEPHONE +44 7950694204 / +44 7885550314

UGANDA

AVAILABLE IN ALL MAJOR BOOK SHOPS